Not Alone

GOD'S PRESENCE ON THE PATH OF THE SPECIAL NEEDS MOM

BY ERICA KINGSBURY

Not Alone

Table of Contents

To Jack,

For showing me the path less traveled and all the joy and beauty awaiting us on it.

To Everett, Jack, and Claire,

Through every season and every path you take, may you always know the hope and love of Jesus and remember that in Him you are never alone.

To Craig,

For telling me to go for it long before I ever did, I aspire to see myself the way you see me. Thank you for sharing this life with me, for being an amazing dad to our three, and for being an incredible husband for me. I love you.

If you are a special needs mom with a recent diagnosis for your child, you're in the right place.

Also, if you're a special needs dad, the grandparent of a special needs child, or even a parent without a special needs child, you can still find an incredible, hope-filled message that might speak to you in a way you weren't expecting.

So, welcome, and keep reading as I share my own story of grappling with the unexpected diagnosis for my child and the journey that has followed.

Introduction: The Unexpected Path

The news I was not expecting to receive rattled me to the core, making me feel like the ground beneath me shifted. I thought I might fall through a black hole of fear and despair.

Such is how I felt upon learning of my son Jack's life-changing diagnosis of William's Syndrome.

The William's Syndrome Association website says, "Williams syndrome is caused by the spontaneous deletion of 26-28 genes on chromosome #7 at the time of conception. The deletion can occur in either the egg or the sperm. It is likely that in most families, the child with Williams syndrome is the only one to have the elastin gene condition in his or her entire extended family.

"It is characterized by medical problems, including cardiovascular disease, developmental delays, and learning challenges. These often occur side by side with striking verbal abilities, highly social personalities, and an affinity for music. WS occurs equally in males and females and in all cultures worldwide" (William's Syndrome Association, 2024).

This diagnosis was completely unexpected and a drastic shift from my original thoughts—that whatever reason Jack was missing milestones and acting so differently than I had ever anticipated, it wasn't due to something this life-changing. I assumed that he would grow out of whatever held him back. Or that everything would be resolved with the proper therapies and interventions. But this diagnosis swept those thoughts and assumptions from my grasp, freeing them to drift away like a balloon floating up into the sky, never to be within reach again. Instead, the concrete, unmoving evidence of a life-altering diagnosis lay at my feet.

It was a complex season of conflicting emotions. I wanted to draw inward and hug myself tight while ignoring my new reality. I was also reaching, with outstretched arms, toward something to hold onto, something to rescue me from drowning in grief.

Life suddenly felt unrecognizable, as did I as I caught glimpses of puffy eyes and swollen, tear-stained cheeks in the mirror.

If any of this sounds familiar to how you've felt or are feeling now, my friend, you are not alone. I've been there, too, and I am here to be that hand that catches you before you fall into the pit of despair. If you've already fallen and are camped down deep in your pit of grief, I'll bring the light, a ladder, and a steady hand to help you climb back out.

Your world might look slightly different than before. You might feel as though you've landed in an unknown world, and, like a stranger in a foreign land, you don't quite grasp the life moving on around you.

If you feel or have felt any of that, I get you. I really get you because that was me, too.

You see, learning of my son's diagnosis was life-shattering. What I once knew to be true about my child and myself was now lying as bits and pieces on the floor, broken, just as I felt at that moment. Maybe you feel that way now as well.

Like a snow globe, my world had just been turned upside down and given a good shake. But instead of a happy little figure skater or a family snuggled into a winter sled, a magical flurry of snowflakes dancing all around them, I felt as if each piece of my world had been catastrophically shaken and was now blowing all around me in chaos. Maybe that's a familiar feeling to you now as well.

We had a vision for our child, his future and ours, and it felt so promised, so secure. But the things of this life are constantly wavering before us, never the guarantee we hope it to be.

Before I knew my son had a disability, I imagined such specific things for his future. When I realized the planned future was not the one in store for us, I felt such a complete loss, as if the very fibers of my existence had been ripped to shreds.

All my sensitive edges were frayed, and I could barely see the hopeful future I once imagined for my son and us as a family. Life as I knew it was now shattered; bits and pieces of it were left jagged at my feet. I felt hopeless about what to do next.

As I stood among the wreckage, grief became the unwelcome guest my heart could not shake. Grief filled the unknowns with worst-case scenario possibilities; whether or not any of them would ever come true, my weary soul had no defense against them.

As parents, we want the best for our children, including their health, happiness, and future. When we realize that a diagnosis may jeopardize those things, it can cause a multitude of emotions to emerge, including fear, grief, and anxiety, just to name a few.

I've grieved for my son, both in the here and now and for what may lie ahead in the future. This type of grief, called anticipatory grief, means that we might grieve for something that hasn't happened yet, such as grieving for the future he may not have or what may be lacking from it, including a driver's license, a college education, marriage, a family, or true independence.

I vividly remember grieving for my three-year-old boy at the time we learned of his diagnosis of William's Syndrome while also grieving for the young man he may not become. Or the freedom of becoming empty-nesters that my husband and I may never know.

Grief can be all-consuming at times. While we may find peace over what we once grieved, there is always something new to grieve as our journey unfolds—another missed milestone we had such high hopes for, another typical childhood activity our son isn't interested in or capable of. How is a parent to handle this?

How can we shoulder our grief and all the other emotions we've now been burdened with as we step into these roles as special needs parents? Will the grief ever end?

We are no strangers to life spinning outside of the expectations we had for it and for sweeping us beyond the limits of pain we assumed were there, keeping us safe from experiencing such hardship. We now have a deeper glimpse into the fragility of life and what we thought we had control over through our son's diagnosis.

Therefore, we must place our hope in something that cannot be destroyed or taken from us and has no limits.

But where can we find such limitless hope and limitless love? Only in Jesus. Like a well that never runs dry, Jesus's love, hope, and peace are meant for you. In walking with Him, we can also find joy, grace, and strength in the challenge of our journey as special needs moms.

If you've ever felt overcome by the grief of your child's diagnosis and felt the heavy weight of fear pressing down upon you, this message of hope is for you.

If you've ever wondered how to be at peace with this new, unknown journey, this message of discovering the peace of Jesus is for you.

If you're feeling robbed of joy these days, you can seek the joy of knowing and loving Jesus. Let's discover how His joy is like the dawn, never failing to rise, even after the coldest, darkest night.

We might have reasons to grieve and fear the unknown, but let us not limit ourselves to those feelings alone. Let us rejoice as we rise above them, born upon wings of grace as we experience the ultimate rescue from our despair.

Jesus, the only true light of this world, can outshine any darkness we face. He is our true Rescuer and Redeemer.

As we grapple with this new diagnosis, we might be tempted to wonder why God would allow our child to face this particular struggle, monumental in its likely hardship and possible limitations.

But God does not have limits on what He can do or create.

"For You formed my inward parts; You covered me in my mother's womb. I will praise You, for I am fearfully and wonderfully made. Marvelous are Your works, and that my soul knows very well" (Psalm 139:13-14).

FINDING STRENGTH AND HOPE IN GOD'S PLAN

This scripture is true for us all, including our neurodiverse children. Maybe we don't understand why God created them with these unique needs, but we can trust that God knew what He was doing.

On this side of heaven, we must hold much of what we know and all our questions with an open hand, trusting everything will make sense one day.

Initially, I felt such a shock from my son's diagnosis, as it took me by complete surprise and threw me off course. The journey I realized I was on was not one I was prepared for or, if I'm being honest, not one I wanted to be on. But learning to walk closer with Jesus unveiled the beauty of this new journey and a strength for the difficult paths along its way.

I also have a new vision for our future that extends far beyond the original boundaries of my imagination: one that reshapes who I thought my son, our family, our future, and I were. This new journey I have found myself on has stretched, strengthened, and transformed me beyond what I could have ever thought I was capable of enduring.

This unique journey is soul-wrenching and life-changing, but it can also be magnificently redeeming if you seek the very One who is the true Redeemer.

God, in His limitless love for us, sent His son, Jesus, to die on the cross for us, to rescue us once and for all from sin. With our faith in Jesus and acceptance of His sacrifice on the cross, we have eternity with Him to look forward to in heaven. Therefore, the challenges we face on earth cannot conquer us. Not even this diagnosis of our son's will have the final say. What a triumph to celebrate!

Let's journey together through these pages, seeking what Scripture says about God's love for us and embracing it to find hope, joy, peace, and strength as we take on these new, brave, and rewarding roles as special needs moms.

And, most importantly, know that you are not alone.

CHAPTER ONE

The Discouragement of the Diagnosis

I magine for a moment you are walking along a path you are familiar with and sure of, and then, in a split second, you helplessly witness in disbelief as the ground before you falls away. Just moments before, solid, walkable ground stood where a giant crevasse had now formed. As you gaze across to the other side, desperate to find a way to keep moving in the direction you thought you were headed, you can see there is no bridge, no path around, and no way to continue onto what you thought was your intended journey.

Receiving a diagnosis for your child feels a lot like standing before an endless chasm, halting your steps at the edge of a steep and rocky cliff as you frantically search for another route around.

It cannot be this way, you think to yourself. Not my child, not me, not this.

But the monstrosity of space between where you stand now and where you thought you would be makes it very clear. You are no longer headed in the direction you always thought you would be on this journey of motherhood.

You might feel left behind, forgotten, and unable to find your way. You might not even see that over there, a little off in the distance, there is something new. Something foreign, much different than you had ever imagined, but it might be beautiful. You wonder if the faint sound of laughter is coming from over there.

As you eventually decide to move toward that far-off direction, to what is new, terrifying, and slightly exciting, you can't help but look back across the chasm you will never cross. You can't help but spill tears for a place you will never know, even though you've always longed to go and know so many others there now.

But as you draw nearer to your new destination, you begin to notice others making this same trek alongside you. Could this be not so bad after all?

My friend, it can be so hard to receive that diagnosis for your child. I vividly remember my pain from the day I found out my son Jack has a rare genetic syndrome called William's Syndrome, soon after celebrating my birthday.

A Devastating Diagnosis

Sitting in a chair at home, wine glass in hand, with tear-stained cheeks and red eyes, I wasn't ending my thirty-fifth birthday as I had imagined I would.

My husband, Craig, kissed my forehead and said goodnight, but there were a million unsaid things between us.

He, too, was reeling from such news, I was sure. But we were undoubtedly processing it differently. He seemed calm while I felt relinquished to the inner chaos of the news as I spiraled into a deep grief.

Just hours before, I sat across from a friend as we wrapped up my birthday dinner. As my husband loaded our two boys into the car and I stayed behind a few moments to say goodbye to my friend, I asked her what felt like an easy question. A question I thought I knew the answer to. However, my question and her answer were about to change everything.

But let's back up a bit in my story for some background on what led to this question in the first place.

During a challenging season of life, I began to think something was amiss with my youngest son.

Besides the constant crying and overall fussiness, he didn't eat well, sleep well, or hit milestones, and, most of all, my mama instincts had been holding up a red flag for months. My youngest son, Jack, was acting so differently than what I had been used to with his older brother, Everett, who is two and a half years older. We all know that each baby is different, but this was *entirely* different.

Eventually, I made a parent referral to the birth-to-three early intervention services program through our state.

As we all suspected, my son presented global delays and qualified for therapy services.

Ultimately, we believed Jack needed extra time to learn things, that he would eventually catch up with his peers and would go on to live the normal life we expected for him.

We were confident of this. My mind had accepted that Jack needed special services and extra time, but I had not entertained the idea that it was anything beyond that.

And while we were still searching for an answer, I wasn't expecting anything "life-changing."

Circling back to where we started in this story, we met a friend for my birthday dinner. She had experience working with special needs children, and I was confident she might have some answers regarding his development. During many of our previous conversations, I'd asked her about getting Jack tested for autism spectrum disorder. Although we thought an ASD diagnosis unlikely for Jack, we felt lost on where to go next and thought, if anything, getting him tested might provide some answers or next steps.

As my husband loaded the boys in the car, I casually asked her what she thought about getting Jack tested.

"So, tell me what you think. Do you think it's autism? Because we don't really think it is," I prompted.

She paused, looked at me, and began slowly, "No, I don't think it is autism. But I think I know what it is, and I'm not sure I want to tell you right now."

She said not right now because of my birthday. And not right now, I can now see, because, at that moment, my friend knew I was happy but unaware.

But reality couldn't wait. And after so much searching, it was time—birthday or not.

And so, with my prompting, she continued, "I believe Jack has William's Syndrome. Have you ever heard of it?"

It wasn't the answer I expected—or hoped for. I was hoping for confirmation that I was right, that he would grow out of it all. And yet, as I had never heard of "William's Syndrome", I did not immediately assume the worst. I only felt grateful she seemed to know what we didn't and was thankful for her insight.

With her goodbye fresh in my ear, I went to the car and quickly searched "William's Syndrome" on Google. Scrolling through my search results, the reality of what I had just learned online started to creep in. The bubble of ignorance now popped; my heart began to deflate in grief.

I read outdated articles that spoke of mental retardation, about adults who don't live independently, don't drive, and can't have jobs with this condition. I read about children with life-threatening cardiovascular problems and the risks of anesthesia during surgery.

As mentioned before, William's Syndrome is a rare genetic condition that happens spontaneously at conception and is characterized by mental and developmental delays, learning disabilities, and unique physical disabilities, including the potential for cardiovascular issues, the most common of which is Supra Valvular Aortic Stenosis, which is when the aorta narrows, and surgical intervention becomes necessary. Adding to the risk of surgery is the fact that those with William's Syndrome can be adversely affected by anesthesia, and it can be life-threatening. All of this I would come to learn and understand through my own at-home research and the countless conversations with medical specialists that followed Jack's official diagnosis, which came about three months after we first heard the term "Williams Syndrome."

But in those first moments, reading all that I found online as we drove home didn't feel real. My husband was calmly beside me, seemingly unphased by everything I told him as I read. "At least we know," he said, his voice tinged with relief.

None of it made any sense to me, though. None of it felt like a relief.

But there, amid all the data, were pictures—pictures of children with William's Syndrome, all looking as if they could be the siblings of our son Jack.

Since Jack was born, we wondered which of us he favored the most. Our oldest son is like the spitting image of both my husband and me. But with Jack, the resemblance was hard to find.

That night, I learned why. The deletion of the elastin chromosome resulted in specific facial features: wide-set eyes, upturned noses, wide smiles, and spaced-apart teeth.

Those adorable little boys and girls from all over the world could pass as a sibling or, in some cases, a twin to my son.

And while it was a shock, it was also heartbreakingly reassuring to know something. Yet, I was still filled with grief.

After that night of reading about William's Syndrome, I cried for a week straight. Everything felt shattered, and I was ill-equipped to put it back together.

It was nothing like I had anticipated. For me, becoming a special needs parent was an abrupt transition. One day, I wasn't, and the next, I was. It felt like an unexpected plunge on a roller coaster I never saw coming.

What I felt was grief and then guilt for the grief. I now know that grief is an essential part of our special needs journey, but it doesn't make you a bad mom, ungrateful, or weak to grieve. It's part of the healing process, even when healing feels far away.

Jesus Sees Your Pain

One of my favorite stories from the New Testament, from the Gospel of John, is when Lazarus dies and his sisters, Mary and Martha, come out to greet Jesus, who arrives in town after the death of Lazarus. Mary is weeping, and Jesus weeps with her. Now, 2,000 plus years later, we know that Jesus isn't going to let Lazarus stay dead for long, but in that moment, Jesus grieves with Mary. Mary, who is likely struggling to make sense of it all and beside herself with grief, is in a puddle of tears, and Jesus, His own heart likely breaking for her, weeps with her.

Can you imagine Jesus grieving alongside you in your situation? In our sadness, despair, and grief, we can crumble at the feet of Jesus and know that He lovingly holds space for our grief, slobbery, snotty tears, and all.

As God knows what we do not, Jesus was keenly aware of the miracle He was about to perform in raising Lazarus from the dead, and there would soon be rejoicing rather than sadness for Mary and Martha. But in those tender moments, He met them where they were, in their despair and pain. Even though Jesus knows the whole of your story and that this diagnosis is not the end but rather the beginning of something entirely more beautiful and miracle-driven than you can comprehend, He still meets you in the place you are at now, in your despair and pain.

Psalm 34:18 says, "The Lord is near to those who have a broken heart," and that is such a comfort to us broken-hearted mamas who are devastated by a medical diagnosis we didn't want nor expect for our children.

As believers, we know the comforts of this world are deceitful and fleeting and cannot satisfy our deepest and greatest needs. Therefore, we must seek comfort from the very One who brings us joy in the morning, no matter how long and dark the night before. His light will always be a light unto our paths (Psalm 30:5; Psalm 119:105).

Unfortunately, it's so easy to feel lost and forgotten as we find ourselves in a new world, one we are barely getting used to as we moms grapple with the medical diagnosis of our children. In those early days, weeks, or months, grief can feel as though it has permanently perched on our shoulders, overshadowing all hope.

Psalm 139 has been my long-time favorite scripture passage, both for myself and my disabled son. I particularly like verse three, which says, "You comprehend my path and my lying down, and are acquainted with all my ways."

It is comforting to know God knows the way, even when I feel clueless about how to proceed. Realizing that it makes perfect sense to God when I struggle to make sense of it all is reassuring.

He has already sorted it out.

He has already overcome the struggle and provided a way for me.

King David writes, "You have hedged me behind and before, and laid Your hand upon me" (Psalm 139:5).

So, while we often feel entirely defeated by this diagnosis, our God, in His limitless love for us, has gone before us, the path for us already forged. And isn't that just what a protective, helpful, and loving Father would do?

In your grief, bring Him your tears and sadness.

In your despair, bring Him your anger and questions.

In your discouragement, bring Him your fears and doubts.

Lay it all before Him, the crumbled mess of shattered dreams. Empty your broken heart to Him so He can rebuild it with healing and hope in His own perfect time and in His beautiful way.

What we see as broken pieces of life, is not too unbroken for God. Limitations or boundaries do not bind Him. You might look in the mirror and see someone you don't recognize, but God sees the real you, the you who will find your stride again.

You are not left behind, forgotten, or helpless, even though it might feel that way now. Help is here. It's here with you now as you hold the very pages of this book, and it's here with you as God gently whispers to you, as He did long ago to Abram, "Do not be afraid, Abram, I am your shield, your exceedingly great reward" (Genesis 15:1).

You are His precious daughter, whom He loves dearly, and He wants you to draw near to Him so that He can be a light on your path, heal your shattered heart, and provide hope that will soothe your soul.

Not Alone in this Journey

If only we were sitting across from one another, mugs of coffee warming our hands and a box of Kleenex between us, nestled into the cozy corner of a coffee shop or tucked into the arms of my living room couch, I'd ask you to share your diagnosis story with me, as I am sharing mine with you.

While our stories might differ greatly, I'm sure we would share knowing smiles and tender tears for the feelings we have both likely felt: joy and grief, discouragement and relief—all mixed and mingled in a way that brings both clarity and confusion.

Like me, you might feel relief for finally having answers, but find that while relief blew in with the diagnosis, it brought with it the unexpected and unwelcome guest we all face on this path: grief.

We are brokenhearted mamas, grieving the loss of what we thought we had. Grieving for who our kids won't be and the multitude of challenges and struggles they will face. Our hearts ache for what lies ahead for them and for us.

As our hearts knit together for shared joys and grief, and our eyes fill with fresh tears, let us remember this truth: He is near.

"The Lord is close to the brokenhearted and saves those who are crushed in spirit" (Psalm 34:18, NASB).

It's a truth we must wear like helmets and carry as shields, protecting our minds and hearts on this journey. This endeavor is not what we expected, but as long as we stick with Him, He will guard and guide us along the way.

I know you are feeling or have felt discouragement since learning of your child's diagnosis, but I'm here to tell you that there is joy in this journey, too. A joy that will quench our thirsty souls and drained hearts, so lovingly designed by a Father who offers us a well that never runs dry.

"Jesus answered and said to her, 'Whoever who drinks of this water will thirst again, but whoever drinks of the water that I shall give him will never thirst. But the water that I shall give him will become in him a fountain of water springing up into everlasting life'" (John 4:13-14).

This journey often feels long, hard, and exhausting. But when your legs tire and your soul fatigues, repeat after me: He is near, He is near, He is near.

Reflect and Pray

1.   What word best describe how you feel since learning of your child's diagnosis?

2.   What are some things you are grieving over the most?

Gather all of those answers from the above questions, whether you write them down, think of them, or speak them out loud, and then imagine yourself laying them at the feet of Jesus.

Just as Mary did, allow yourself to fall at His feet in your grief and know that He meets you right where you are.

Our pain, our grief, the struggles we have—none of them surprises Him.

Remember, grieving is not a sign of weakness but a way to process the deep, complicated, heavy emotions that you feel.

On more than one occasion, I have found myself having a good cry, which is just a way of saying that I let loose and allowed myself to sob. And, in the end, the way I felt after could be called "good." As my mom used to say when I was younger, and especially as I entered my teen years and emotions began to get bigger, "Sometimes, you just need a good cry." And she was right, of course.

Now as a mom of three young children, one with a disability, I often find myself letting those tears roll as I cry out to God, mixing my weeping with worship. It never ceases to help me feel better and better, and I feel closer to God by inviting Him into my grief.

How might you be able to invite God into the grief you feel? You could start by telling Him about it in prayer, journaling about it, or, like my mom's wise advice, having a good cry with Him.

However you choose to invite Him in, God meets you there.

A Prayer for the Mom with a New Diagnosis for Her Child

Heavenly Father, I come to you with a broken heart, devastated by this diagnosis for my child. I am shattered by this news, confused, worried, anxious for answers, and fearful for the future. I'm also grieving the loss of the life I thought my child would have and that I would have as their mother.

I ask for Your peace, comfort, and guidance as I navigate this new journey. I know You are always with me, and You see me in this difficult time.

I know You have a beautiful plan for our lives, and I trust You completely, even when I don't understand.

Help me to draw nearer and nearer to You. Thank you for Your unending love and Your presence in my life.

In the precious and holy name of Jesus, Amen.

CHAPTER TWO

Discovering Joy

Recently, I tucked my boys into their beds in their shared room. The black-out curtains were pulled together, the lights turned off, and their favorite stuffies and blankets were nestled under an arm or close to a pillow.

It had been a tough day at home for us all. The developmental delays caused by William's Syndrome caused Jack to act more like a toddler than his actual five years of age. A recent ADHD diagnosis provided greater insight into Jack, but it also introduced a new set of challenging behaviors, making everyday life feel like a monumental struggle.

The constant arguing.

The whining and complaining.

The impulsivity that created sibling fights and shed tears.

His obsession with constantly watching TV.

His destructive tendencies left little bits and pieces of toys, batteries, and screws strewn about as he enjoyed taking apart any toy—his or his siblings—it didn't matter. Just as long as he could gleefully disassemble something.

His lack of comprehension of rules, playing fair, or sharing.

Barging into his sister's room while she lay sleeping for a nap, waking her up and pushing me beyond the brink of frustration.

Constant movement, from jumping to kicking, running and grabbing, dropping toys throughout the house, all while yelling and shrieking to release his energy in ways that made sense to him but disrupted and overstimulated the rest of us.

Toys and crumbs from his constant movement littered every room of the house, and sticky fingers created sticky surfaces, leaving a trail for me to follow with a cleaning rag.

His inability to play independently or imaginatively demands a constant stream of entertainment, built from loud noises like the continuous thump and slap of dribbling a basketball throughout the house or repeatedly listening to the same high-pitched song from a toy I was plotting to steal the batteries from.

Desperate to get through the day with even a shred of peace and sanity, I tried to pick my battles. At the end of most days, exhausted and burnt out, I surveyed the damage done by my incredibly active little boy and felt defeated.

Often, it felt overwhelming for all of us. I, in particular, felt the weight the most, becoming burnt out and weary.

Some days are like that with a child who operates in a world different from ours, even though our feet rest in the same shared space. Through his lens, what he wants, he takes. What he needs, he needs right now, at this very instant. What seems small to me is an earth-shattering, world-ending big deal to him. What might feel or sound soothing to him is the opposite for me; I might as well be scraping my nails along a chalkboard.

It makes for long days for me, him, and everyone in the family.

On this specific day, I was irritable and angry at the swings this diagnosis of William's Syndrome and ADHD was taking at me. Jack had always presented with challenging behaviors, from his colicky beginning as a baby to his fussiness as a toddler. I'd grown accustomed to Jack's high needs, yet my patience was nowhere to be found like the Legos and Nerf darts lost and forgotten within the couch cushions.

I tried my best, but ultimately I lost my cool too many times, yelled to get Jack's attention, threatened in anger about taking away favorite toys, and was overall a miserable mom.

Not at all filled with joy.

After we said our prayers that night, and I felt a weary sigh come from my heart as the familiar presence of guilt let itself in, I held Jack in my arms and covered his cheeks and nose with kisses, like an offering of a thousand "I'm sorrys" and "I love yous."

He snuggled deeper into my arms, said I was his sweetheart, and loved me so much, cracking right through the hard shell of irritability and frustration I'd built myself in throughout the day.

How can someone so small have such a profound impact on me, breaking the iron walls of discouragement I've built around myself with a simple snuggle and an "I love you"?

His little head on my chest, his tiny arms squeezing tightly around my neck, his whisper of "You're my girl," and I'm no longer the hard-hearted, over-stimulated, unemotionally regulated wreck I was just moments before.

How can we live with hardship and find joy? How do we stand among the rubble of our lives, start putting things back together, and be joyful about it while doing so?

As I moved over to Everett's bed, my oldest son, I also began with an apology. I was sorry for how rough the day had been and recognized how unfair this might feel to him, the older brother of a child with a disability who often made for hard days.

And with effortless wisdom well beyond his eight years, his response triggered the sting of tears in my eyes and swept the air from my chest.

"Mom, you don't need to worry or apologize. Some days are just hard. And you couldn't ask for a more perfect second son than Jack. Because God wanted him to be yours, and God wanted you for Jack. It's just the way it's supposed to be."

In his simple yet profoundly true statement, I felt my mindset do a 180.

This is just how it is supposed to be.

This freshly served wisdom from an eight-year-old son got me thinking about how often I grapple with what's supposed to be and what I wish could be. Like a blinking, neon sign, the realization that I would have more joy if I wrestled with my situation less was hard to miss.

Joy in the Climb

What I had been trying to push against wasn't meant to be moved. This mountain was mine to climb, not just for the steep and rocky paths but also for the incredible, unparalleled views it could offer me.

And as if the clouds and fog surrounding the mountain I was clinging to were lifted, clarity settled in within me.

Joy is not meant to be absent during hardships. So often, the trek of the climb itself produces a joyful sense of purpose and accomplishment as you gain altitude and push through the most complicated parts.

The book of Proverbs advises that "A merry heart does good, like medicine, but a broken spirit dries up the bones" (Proverbs 17:22).

King David writes, "If I say, 'My foot slips,' Your mercy, O Lord, will hold me up. In the multitude of my anxieties within me, Your comforts delight my soul" (Psalm 94:18-19).

We can find true joy even amid our struggles if we seek it from the true joy-giver, God. When we consider all that God has done, from the beginning of His creation to the redemption through the cross, we can fill our hearts with joy for today and hope for tomorrow.

Like the fresh mountain air, as we climb our mountains of trials, the joy of the Lord can fill our lungs with each breath we take. It's that accessible.

Embracing Joy in this Journey

I'm sometimes asked how we got beyond the diagnosis and how we have adapted since.

It's a delicate dance, my friend. Some days, I know the steps well, and I sing along with the moves, adding some extra sway to my confident steps. On other days, I stumble on two left feet, completely blindsided by new choreography.

Accepting that Jack is who God meant for him to be, *with a disability,* is sometimes easier said than done. My head often gets it, but my heart is still tripping up, looking back and wondering what could have been.

This feeling reminds me of Lot's wife.

The woman turned into a salt statue because her heart held her back. She knew she needed to leave her home, but her heart said otherwise, which didn't go well for her in the end (Genesis 19:26).

Finding the courage to not look back upon what you are leaving behind or what might have been is nearly always a heart issue. Our eyes follow the direction of our hearts.

My deceitful heart will always wander toward my ideals and expectations, my dreams and hopeful realities for Jack.

But what about God's heart?

What direction would my eyes gaze if I aligned my heart with His?

True joy does not come from what this world offers. This world can offer us moments of happiness, but joy is not a fleeting feeling. Joy is something we can hold onto, even when the storms of our lives rage around us.

The Bible clearly states that we should be joyful during times of hardship.

In the book of James, we read, "My brethren, count it all joy when you fall into various trials, knowing that the testing of your faith produces patience" (Jame 1: 2-3).

Have you ever wrestled with this pursuit of joy the way I have? Knowing that we are served an extra heap of hardships as we navigate the difficulties of raising a child with special needs? Have you ever felt doomed to fail at keeping your joy because life with this diagnosis is hard?

God, who loves us, allows us to walk through trials, knowing that we can persevere and that incredible growth awaits us through the trial and at the end. And as a loving God, He does not leave us alone in those trials.

I love this passage from the book of Isaiah: "When you pass through the waters, I will be with you; and when you pass through the rivers, they will not sweep over you. When you walk through the fire, you will not be burned; the flames will not set you ablaze" (Isaiah 43:2, NIV)

We can find joy in trials because we have a loving Father whom we can trust to see us through.

We can find joy in Him now and in the hope of eternity.

When I choose to place my joy and all hope in the Lord, recognizing that whatever happens in this earthly life is not the final chapter, it brings me great joy.

When I remember that a storm doesn't last forever and that God is there with me, a clap of booming thunder is but a whisper.

When I am losing my patience at home with my children, am growing weary from the mundane, or am grappling with the realities of my child's diagnosis, I can turn to the One who says, "Fear not, for I am with you" (Isaiah 43:5), and find joy in His presence and promises.

As I started a new day with my kids, following the one I'll always tally into the "hard mom days" category, my mind was clear, and my heart was full.

Not of anxiety or annoyance.

But of love and joy.

Love for my special needs son and all of my children, and joy for the role I was hand-picked by God to do.

With my heart aligned with God and my eyes lining up with His vision, not mine, I can see something I could have never seen before—something beautiful and miraculous I would have missed if I were set on following the ways of my own heart.

This is a special role just for me, with some of the steepest climbs I've ever encountered and the most breathtaking, soul-lifting views I've ever witnessed.

Jack's diagnosis may have been the hammer that made my world collapse, but my joy in the Lord has pieced it back together and reconstructed the walls of my heart, creating space for everything new that I didn't know before.

And with God's presence in my heart, and through all I face in this life, joy blooms and strengthens me.

We CAN Have Joy in Our Hearts

There is a song my kids often come home from Sunday school singing. As our car fills with the chorus of little voices from the back seat, this one line in particular sticks in my head for the rest of the day.

"I've got the joy, joy, joy, joy down in my heart" (Cooke, 1925).

When I think of joy being down in my heart, it makes me think of tree roots deep in the soil. I live in an area where the wind blows quite a lot, so high winds are not uncommon, ranging from twenty to sixty miles per hour. Many of our trees have stood for decades and have not been taken down by a fierce wind blowing at them. So, those tree roots must be strong and deep, keeping the tree from being uprooted by such a violent force.

If only I were a tree and could withstand such forces in my own life, maybe I could stay more upright when life's challenges whip me around like a strong wind, aiming to knock me over.

Raising a child with a special needs diagnosis might feel like a vicious wind trying to push you down, but like those tall trees, if we plant ourselves in the right soil and allow ourselves to grow, we, too, can stand tall and strong—and joyful.

That right soil comes from time with God and reading His word. The more I do those things, the more my roots grow. Because, in Him, all the things He has set before me are things I can withstand (Philippians 4:13).

The more I grow my own roots and stand stronger, the more I can help my family grow and stand tall and strong, too. Our joy need not depend on circumstances alone, as joy can be fully present and accessible in any obstacle we face. Our joy is such because it comes from a living God who will walk with us daily, who does not withhold His goodness, and who always keeps His promises.

And in Him, there is fullness of joy (Psalm 16:11).

Reflect and Pray

Galatians 5:22-23 (ESV) says, "But the fruit of the Spirit is love, joy, peace, patience, kindness, goodness, faithfulness, gentleness, self-control; against such things, there is no law."

These attributes are listed as "fruit of the Spirit," meaning they are produced in us when we walk by the Spirit. In other words, when we walk with Jesus and are faithful to Him, living according to the way He has called us to live, we will be transformed by the Holy Spirit.

And as a result of us doing this?

More love, *joy,* peace, patience, kindness, goodness, faithfulness, gentleness, and self-control.

It doesn't say our circumstances will change, but our hearts will. The transformation of our hearts that comes from a daily walk with Jesus is how we grow to bear such fruit.

Doesn't such fruit sound like lovely attributes to have as we journey on as moms to our rare and special children?

Reflect on how you can walk more in the Spirit, more closely with Jesus, and then in prayer, ask Him for help in doing so.

1. **Be honest. In what ways do you feel that your child's diagnosis has stolen your joy?**

2. **In what ways have you found joy since learning of your child's diagnosis?**

A Prayer for Embracing Joy
Along the Journey

Heavenly Father, I admit that it is often difficult to find joy in the journey I am now on. But I know that with Christ in me, I can have abundant joy.

I ask for the Holy Spirit to lead me in a closer walk with You, God, that I may bear more fruit, that of love, joy, peace, patience, kindness, goodness, faithfulness, gentleness, and self-control.

I ask for You to open the eyes of my heart to witness the joyful moments all around me, even when I am still struggling with the news of my child's diagnosis.

I thank you for the gift of my child and all that they bring to my life, and that You have chosen me to be their mom.

In the precious and holy name of Jesus, Amen.

CHAPTER THREE

Shattered Dreams

Sweat began to gather and drip, tickling its way down my back underneath the turtleneck sweater I regretted wearing as I held my four-year-old son with all my strength.

It was my older son Everett's first school Christmas program, and everyone was there, from teachers and students to parents, grandparents, friends, and community members. The gymnasium of our small school was full of people and noise as everyone around us talked and laughed, like a cheerful hum that filled the air with a merriness fitting for the season.

As the parents of a first-grader, we had chosen to sit near the front and in the center of the crowd for the best view of our smiling, singing student when it was his turn to stand with his class and perform their familiar Christmas tunes.

As a new-ish family of five, my husband held our infant daughter while I sat with Jack on my lap. Jack's excitement and energy built as his patience and ability to sit still collapsed into what I could sense drove us straight toward meltdown territory.

I kept a firm handle on him while the music began, a jolly sound that, unfortunately, irritated his sensitive ears and heightened his restlessness.

I could sense his agitation and anticipated his movements, trying to keep him from breaking free of my arms and bolting for what he wanted most.

A pile of fake, wrapped Christmas presents lay nestled under a fake Christmas tree, creating part of the performance's background.

And Jack, thinking the presents were real, wanted them very badly.

I tried to enjoy this first school Christmas program, but instead, I felt like I was in charge of keeping a ticking time bomb from going off at any moment.

When the last song concluded, the crowd cheered and clapped. Jack slipped out of my hands as I stood to gather our things and immediately sprinted away from me. As if the wall of a dam lifted, and the waters spilled forth, so did the crowd, as students and parents became a sea of bodies, and I could not find Jack.

But I knew where he was going.

Christmas presents.

I reached him just as he began tearing into that first package. And then it was over. Screaming and kicking, I picked him up and scanned the sea of faces for my husband. As I darted from one set of eyes to another, I finally found his eyes as he found mine. With our calm and happy daughter in his arms and our overstimulated, raging son in mine, we looked at one another with understanding and instantly made a wordless decision.

We were leaving.

While the evening's events had yet to conclude, Jack's meltdown abruptly ended the evening for our family and we needed to leave.

As we left, I could not help but notice the sea of faces take on familiar looks: looks of compassion, understanding, shock, and, worst of all, disapproval.

As we pulled my oldest from his friends, said our quick goodbyes to family members, and walked past the lighted Christmas parade trucks parked outside the school, I felt the heaviness of disappointment settle into my chest.

At that moment, I believed it would always be this hard. It would always be leaving events early, disappointing my other children, and dragging a screaming child through a room while others shamed and judged me.

I felt unqualified for this role of special needs mom and defeated by its very nature.

As we drove home early that evening, disappointment felt like a tangible weight on my chest And I felt the sharp sting of my shattered dreams, the ones I had held in my heart as I imagined what life would be like with children. The dream of having three children who could all participate in normal school activities while my husband and I sat and watched now felt so unrealistic.

The hope and expectations of the future for Jack felt like the pages of a book had been violently ripped away. Where a story was supposed to unfold for us was now gone; jagged edges of paper remaining instead.

The questions bouncing around in my mind were a direct link to the fears I had.

Will we ever be able to go somewhere as a family and enjoy ourselves?

Will Jack require more and more assistance throughout life as he gets older?

Will we ever get the opportunity to enjoy being empty-nesters?

Will I forever be a caregiver to my son?

I was eager to find a solution and desperate for it to resemble the "normal" experiences and future I had expected for us all. I felt equipped to be a mom but ill-equipped to be a special needs mom.

Why had God called me to this if I was so unprepared?

God, the Way Maker

In my doubts during that very tender and raw post-diagnosis season, I am reminded of Moses. Moses is one of my favorite Bible characters, as I am drawn to his story regularly when I think about who God has called me to be.

Early in the book of Exodus, we meet Moses, whom God has chosen to become the leader of the Israelites as they flee from Egypt toward the Promised Land. This assignment will require much more from Moses than he imagines he is capable of. We see a beautiful exchange between Moses and God in Exodus 4:10-12:

> Then Moses said to the Lord, "O my Lord, I am not eloquent, neither before nor since You have spoken to your servant; but I am slow of speech and slow of tongue." So the Lord said to him, "Who has made man's mouth? Or who makes the mute, the deaf, the seeing, or the blind? Have not I, the Lord? Now therefore, go, and I will be with your mouth and teach you what you shall say."

Upon hearing directly from God that He has chosen Moses to step into this monumental role, Moses replies in a way many of us will relate to.

Who am I?

Sound familiar?

Even amid the presence of God, Moses can't help but begin this new journey with self-doubt.

Moses's doubts about his abilities to succeed in this new God-designed leadership role are relatable to us, but that's because, like Moses, we see ourselves as limited.

Patient with his doubts and questions, God reminds Moses of who *He* is and that, as the Creator, He can teach the very mouth of Moses to speak in the way God needs him to.

What we see as limits, God can prove to be limitless.

I feel a kinship with Moses, as I, too, have doubted why God chose me for this unique motherhood role. But, like Moses, I am reminded of who God is.

He gives us the words when we don't have them.

He makes a way when there wasn't one before.

He qualifies the unqualified.

We might be staring at the mess of our shattered dreams, overwhelmed by the uncertainty of navigating through them. We might wonder why God has asked us to steward this task.

Moses became a great leader to his people; his initial self-doubts did not hinder God's plan for him.

Our fears and doubts do not have to hold us back, either. We, too, can blossom into the new role we have taken on amid the uncertainty of these new responsibilities. We can trust that God qualifies and equips us for all that lies before us.

How might I handle that Christmas event now instead of how I handled it then years ago?

First, I know much more about my son, what triggers him, what he can handle, and his limitations. I would have chosen a seat near the exit so that one of us, or even a grandparent, could have taken him for a walk down the hallway instead if it became too much. I would have brought his noise-canceling headphones and a fidget toy to keep his attention. I would craft my expectations for the evening around what I now know Jack is capable of, rather than hoping for behavior beyond his abilities.

And I certainly would have gone with something other than a turtleneck sweater.

Unfortunately, it's easy to look back and notice all of my mistakes from those early days, but with grace, I can be tender with myself because I just didn't know all I do now.

The beauty in looking back and reflecting on how far we have come is seeing how God *has* equipped us step by step.

He is faithful in His promises to be with us, no matter how steep and rocky the path becomes. He is trustworthy in teaching and guiding us, while patient with our doubts and fears. He is loving in His care for our broken hearts and thoughtful in how He heals us.

The voice in our head that often booms loudest is that this situation is too hard, it isn't supposed to be this way, and I don't know how to do this.

But listen for the gentle voice, often just a whisper, that says, *I am with you; I will strengthen you; I will help you.*

"Fear not, for I am with you; Be not dismayed, for I am your God. I will strengthen you, yes, I will help you, I will uphold you with My righteous right hand" (Isaiah 41:10).

A shattered dream can make way for a new one, and the journey doesn't have to be navigated with fear and uncertainty but with the grace and love of God.

In our healing, the broken pieces shift and fit together unexpectedly, creating something entirely new.

And perhaps the entirely new thing is us, hand-crafted by our Creator in the breaking and rebuilding to become the stronger, more capable versions of ourselves we were always meant to be.

The version of ourselves that sees the shattering as an awakening.

Sees the rubble as the foundation upon which we rebuild.

Growing stronger with each step we take in this new role, we feel, see, and know that God is equipping and strengthening us, building confidence within us that is born through His amazing grace so that we may steward the task set before us with purpose, peace, and an abundance of new dreams.

For it is often through our shattering that we become strong.

Dreaming New Dreams

I might always be able to vividly recall that Christmas program and the chaos that interrupted and cut the family outing short for us. I'll bet you have a similar moment imprinted in your mind, too. One that crafted questions and doubts that linger in your head, echoing through your thoughts as you wonder if you'll ever get beyond this challenging stage of life.

Since then, my lingering question, like a shadow hiding in the corners of my mind, has been this: Will we ever be able to enjoy life like other families do?

While I have faced this question many times and found a thousand moments of peace, I can't bury the truth. No matter how heavy a weight I can tie to this fearful thought and toss it into the ocean, trying to rid myself of it, it bobs back up, resurfacing in my thoughts because the diagnosis is here to stay.

No matter how I wrestle with it, my son's and our family's truth remains the same.

We are going to experience life differently than I expected.

And just like anything else in life, I find peace when I stop expecting an outcome I know is impossible and embrace the reality before me. Peace for our current reality and our likely future. The peace that enables something that also bobs to the surface as an unexpected and, finally, welcome feeling I am happy to anchor myself to: *enjoyment.*

When I embrace the differences this diagnosis brings into our lives and enjoy the extraordinary view I'm granted because of it, I am free to enjoy my son even more than I already do. I'm free to see his differences as gifts rather than disruptions. While some days are harder than others, and the unknowns and medical complexities still loom before me like a storm threatening to roll in, I can lift my face to the sun and bask in the contentedness it brings.

My friend, my heart breaks for you as you stand among the debris of your shattered dreams. I've been there, too. But from my own experience, new dreams and a new future await when the old dreams are let go. And they are surprising, exciting, and full of hope.

God equips us with each brave step we take into this new, unknown future. And in a way, it is a beautiful shattering, breaking us free from all that holds us back if we were to sit in the grief of what could have been.

It's okay to mourn what you've lost. But when it's time, pick up those broken pieces, and enjoy the way they shift into something beautiful, perhaps something always meant to be just this way.

And be free to dream new dreams.

Reflect and Pray

In this chapter, we reflected on Moses, whom God called to lead the Israelites out of slavery in Egypt and into the Promised Land. As we read in scripture, Moses felt completely unqualified for the task set before him and, I'm guessing, that it likely did not align with the plans he had for his future.

In thinking of Moses's story, I thought of someone else, too.

Mary, the mother of Jesus.

God called upon a young, teenage girl to bring the Savior into the world. What a monumental task set before her! And yet, her faith and love for God overpowered any fears or the hopes and plans she must have had for her future.

"Then Mary said, 'Behold the maidservant of the Lord! Let it be to me according to your word'" (Luke 1:38).

Mary's faithful obedience to God, despite the personal struggles she would inevitably face in her new situation as mother to Jesus, can be an inspiration to us to do the same.

Think of or write down ways that you can have faithful obedience in this new role as a special needs mom and then pray over them.

1. In the wake of your child's diagnosis, what are your shattered dreams? In what ways do you feel that life will be different than you thought it would?

2. In what ways do you feel ill-equipped for this role as a special needs mom?

A Prayer for the Mom with a Heartful of Shattered Dreams

Heavenly Father, I come to you with a long list of hopes and dreams that now feel shattered in light of my child's diagnosis. I fear for my child's future and all the unknowns that I am worried about.

I feel ill-equipped for this role You have called me to, and I can't help but feel overwhelmed at the task set before me.

But like Moses and Mary, I know that You qualify the unqualified and that You are faithful in walking with us along this journey.

I ask for my faith to be strengthened and for space in my heart for new dreams, bigger and better than I could have imagined.

I ask for You to equip me for this role and guide me with Your wisdom as I learn this new role and all that it will require of me.

Thank you for the blessing that is Your word and that we can learn from it.

In the precious and holy name of Jesus, Amen.

CHAPTER FOUR

Strength in Surrender

On a warm, early spring day, I came out of my bedroom with an armful of laundry, which almost landed at my feet when I saw who stood before me. My two boys, dressed alike in cowboy attire, giant smiles on their little faces, readying to go outside and play together.

When my oldest son, Everett, noticed Jack didn't have all the gear he needed, he rushed to wrap a toy holster around his middle. Jack patiently stood while his big brother secured the holster, adjusted the bandana tied around his neck, and offered him a nod of approval.

With a grin that made his sky-blue eyes sparkle, Jack seemed to stand a bit taller at that moment—heightened by more than just the tall boots and hat.

In true mom fashion, I begged them for a picture, and like the gentlemanly cowboys they are, they stood for a few pictures before heading out for a morning of bandit-chasing deputy work on the western frontier.

And it was a joyous morning for us all.

What a dream come to life before my eyes, in all its cowboy hat, oversized boots, and red-and-blue bandana glory.

In grieving through the implications of my son's diagnosis, I've come face to face with reality many times. As my son grows up, the typical milestones are nowhere along our path, and with the harsh reality of a life outside the norm, I have often felt disappointment for the loss of what could have been for our family.

It's as if those shattered dreams lie on the floor, waiting to prick the tender parts of my feet as I tread past them.

But moments like this, watching my boys, so close in age but often so far apart in abilities, run and play together, even if just for a morning, feels like I've found the broom and have set to cleaning up some of those old dreams with their jagged bits strewn about my path. And in my sweeping away those shattered dreams, something new is given the space to bloom and become established.

From time to time, I've considered that my inability to sweep away all those broken hopes and dreams is not because I can't but because I don't want to.

If I clean it all up and toss it away, what then?

Do I have to say goodbye to my once-held hopes for my son?

I could sit and stare at these little broken pieces all day, imagining what could have been until I'm on the floor, just as broken as they are.

As you sift through what feels broken, remember this: There will be moments and glimpses of something new and different, something you cannot look away from because it will feel like a miracle, and the sheer joy of this newness will be like a gentle nudge in the direction you are meant for.

Like two little cowboy hats running through the field together.

It wasn't long after receiving Jack's diagnosis that I read the poem *Welcome to Holland* by Emily Perl Kingsley—a beautifully written description of what it's like raising a child with a disability, especially when it was what you least expected.

In her poem, Kingsley describes getting on a plane to Italy, but instead of landing in Italy, you've landed in Holland and can't return. Everyone you know is in Italy, where you always dreamt you would be.

But you are in Holland, and you must stay there. While it's not as flashy and exciting as Italy, it is beautiful and has some really special and unique attributes. And in time, you realize that you would truly miss it if you had to leave.

She ends her poem with this:

But everyone you know is busy coming and going from Italy .... and they're all bragging about what a wonderful time they had there. And for the rest of your life, you will say, "Yes, that's where I was supposed to go. That's what I had planned." And the pain of that will never, ever, ever, ever go away .... because the loss of that dream is a very significant loss. But ... if you spend your life mourning the fact that you didn't get to Italy, you may never be free to enjoy the very special, the very lovely things .... about Holland. (1987)

When I first read these words, I wasn't quite ready to embrace the beauty of Holland. I spent a lot of time thinking of Italy and what I was missing out on.

But now that I've been in "Holland" for a while, it's where my heart is. A missing piece I never knew existed awaited me in this once-foreign and extra-special land.

We can mourn what we won't get to have or experience. Certainly, it's a crucial part of our journeys, but we've got to lift our heads a little and see that while we aren't where we thought we'd be, there is a rare beauty surrounding us. The more we notice it, the more we recognize it for what it is.

A gift.

Not the diagnosis itself but the child that we are blessed with. They, in their unique and special ways, are the gift. A gift that teaches and pushes us to explore the outer limits of a world many live without ever noticing, but one that we get to witness daily.

The trek of a special needs mom is long and hard, lonely at times, but it's filled with everyday miracles that few can see.

It reminds me of Jesus's disciples and how they were each called away from their respective professions to follow Him. From fishermen to tax collectors, they left something behind to pursue something completely different and unknown.

While the disciples each *chose* to step off their paths and onto a new one, we can find similarities in our journeys as they faced the unknown, witnessed miracles, experienced doubts in their faith, made mistakes, and led lives so rare and unique to those around them.

It's safe to assume that those men never dreamt of all that they would encounter, from the joy of walking alongside Jesus to the teachings they would hear from Him, the miracles they would witness, the persecution they would endure, the devastation of Jesus's death, and the unparalleled joy at His resurrection.

From where we are now, so early in our journeys, let us imagine the incredible joys and miracles that await us. An entirely new future awaits us with our children.

It sure makes me want to grab a broom and get to sweeping, removing all the old dreams that threaten to poke me in the heel and make room for all the new dreams that beckon me toward what lies ahead.

Gathering my shattered hopes and dreams, the very ones I had for my son and what his future might hold: from his future wife to the grandbabies I would get to snuggle; the epic trips he and his brother would take together, most likely backpacking and hunting their way across their favorite states, much like their dad and uncle have done; the phone calls that would come while he was away at college or starting a new job in a new city.

All of those "normal" routes I assumed his life would take, those were my dreams for him.

All of those mama hopes gathered into the palm of my hand, broken dreams shattered into pieces—unsure of what to do with it all.

Because if I let go, I have to surrender it *all*.

And at the thought of surrender, I feel a tug.

A whisper.

A calling.

To surrender my hopes, dreams, and vision for my son, for me, for us, for his sibling relationships, for our family, and for his future.

There is a tension between holding on and letting go, but we must lean into what the Scriptures say about surrendering our plans to God's will to give us the strength to hand it all over to Him.

In Proverbs, scripture encourages us to trust God, not in what we know but in what He knows, submitting our plans to Him so He may make the path straight for us (Proverbs 3:5-6).

We might also be familiar with Jeremiah's words: "For I know the thoughts that I think toward you, says the Lord, thoughts of peace and not of evil, to give you a future and a hope" (Jeremiah 29:11).

We may not understand God's plan for our lives, but as believers, we can trust that He works it all for the good of those who love Him (Romans 8:28).

Letting go feels freeing and terrifying, but I open my hands and surrender it all to God, based on my trust in His promises.

While we may be tempted to hold on to what we think is in our control, or might bring us the most happiness, submission and surrender give us the strength to embrace His plans for us.

In that surrender, we are set free from all the "what could have been" that once bound us.

Unshackled by the weight of shattered dreams, we can provide room for joy, peace, and hope into the future we now see taking shape before us.

Letting Go and Letting God

Tucking Jack in at night is always interesting, to say the least. Just before bedtime, he is often his sweetest and funniest. He wants to snuggle and tell my husband and I how much he loves us, but he also regales us with the funniest one-liners and little stories that he's somehow tucked away all day until just before bed.

As he has gotten older, we've seen more of this side of him come out. He is equal parts sweet and affectionate, hilarious with perfect comedic timing and quite stubborn; it's a wonderful, if not challenging, combination. He is strong-willed to the extreme and will fight every battle he can, but in an instant, he might throw you off balance with a sweet hug or the funniest phrase you've ever heard.

A few years after his diagnosis, as I was seeing more and more of his personality, the characteristics of William's Syndrome, and the notable markers of his learning disability, I was often struggling with him. He was stubborn, hyper-fixated, over-stimulated, and highly emotional as the day went on, struggling with him anywhere we went.

But amid our many rough patches, I began to see glimpses of something incredible—something I wanted more of. I often wished I could reach in and grab hold of what I saw glimmering before me, bringing it to the forefront.

I saw deep compassion and love for others, intelligence, a photographic memory so that he would never forget a face or a name, a sense of humor—the goofiness of any young boy—friendliness, a desire to learn and explore the world around him, and someone who had goals and dreams of his own for his life.

I saw all of these things in and out of focus, as if I were playing with the lens of a camera. It gave me hope that things wouldn't always be this hard with him. That somewhere along the way and with growth, maturity, and us learning how to better serve and meet his unique needs, we would bring those wonderful characteristics more to the surface.

Seeing those pieces of him was like a peek behind the curtain of what was to come. And it filled me with hope, relief, and anticipation.

This will be okay, I said to myself.

I began to imagine the amazing things Jack *would* accomplish. How many milestones and successful endeavors will I get to witness him accomplish? How many times will he blow us all away with what he is capable of? What joy will I know when I see him with a group of friends or working at a job he loves?

Surrendering myself to an unknown future feels hard, while surrendering to a future full of hope is much easier. When I can't see the hope and only see the difficulties, God gives me those little sneak peeks to fuel my hope in such an unknown future— so much so that I can't wait to know it, live it, and love it.

Some days, the surrender is easy, and some days, it is hard, regardless of how many good days I've had. But I keep surrendering because I know His plan is greater.

Join me in seeking His plan, surrounding our own, and looking forward to all that awaits us.

Reflect and Pray

It would be unlikely for most of us to up and leave our jobs and the life we know if someone asked us to.

But that's exactly what the disciples of Jesus did.

I've often glossed over this while reading my Bible, likely because it's a story I've heard over and over from a young age, and I'm used to it. But when I pause and allow myself to stand in their shoes, it hits differently.

Fishermen, a tax collector, a religious warrior: these were some of the lifestyles of the twelve disciples before they started following Jesus.

But then they were called to something different. And interestingly enough, it had nothing to do with their job titles. Instead, it must have had to do with their hearts and their willingness to surrender themselves to walk with Jesus.

As Christ followers, we all want to walk with Jesus and we know that His plans are better than our own. So, then why is it so hard to give up control and surrender ourselves over to Him?

Well, for starters, all of us like to be in control. It's scary when we aren't.

We must learn to trust God over ourselves and the way to do that is to be transformed through Him.

"Therefore, if anyone is in Christ, he is a new creation; old things have passed away; behold, all things have become new" (2 Corinthians 5:17).

Giving our lives to Jesus and surrendering ourselves to Him makes us new. It's a freedom we can step into each and every day.

1.   **What were the plans you had for your child and your life with them? In what ways are you struggling to let go of those plans?**

2.   **What might happen if you were to surrender your plans to God's plans, allowing Him to take control?**

A Prayer for the Mom as She Surrenders it All

Heavenly Father, I am struggling to surrender all of my hopes, worries, fears, and plans to You. I am often guilty of believing that I know best and if I just stay in control, all will be well.

But I know that Your plans are far greater and more rewarding than mine, and that I do want to experience all that You have in store for my child and for me. I know that You love my child more than I can imagine and that You have great things planned for them.

I ask for a more trusting heart when it comes to handing over control of my life and that of my child. I trust You with all of their medical needs and ask for guidance as we learn more about this diagnosis and what their social, emotional, learning, and developmental needs will look like.

Create in me a new heart, God, and transform all of my ways so that I seek more and more to follow You and not my own plans.

I hand over control and surrender to You and Your perfect plan. I pray that in doing so, I will serve You and give You glory.

In the precious and holy name of Jesus, Amen.

CHAPTER FIVE

Faith Under Fire

I stood at the door of my infant son Jack's room with anger rolling off of me. Like a hammer, my heart pounded, and my fingers curled into fists, itching to punch the wall to the beat of the thunder within my chest.

On the other side of the door, my five-month-old lay crying and shrieking in his crib. It was 3:00 a.m., and my eyes had barely rested in the sweet bliss of sleep that night.

I was not angry with my son, not with his tears or his inability to sleep more than an hour at a time.

I was angry with God.

I sent a frustrated cry toward heaven that roared from the depths of my overtired and worn-out soul, *"Why? WHY did You give me such a difficult baby?!"*

In Jack's first six months, the crying was relentless. Nearly every effort to soothe him failed, and I spent most of my days with him strapped to my chest in a Baby Bjorn while I bounced around my house cleaning and also parenting a toddler.

Getting Jack to sleep at night was a three-hour pursuit, and I often paced his pitch-black room and wept as Everett yelled for Mommy on the other side of the door and my husband did his best to carry on the evening without me.

In those days, I wondered when I would witness a sunset again instead of bouncing and shushing a restless baby to sleep for hours each night, entering his room while the sun was up and exiting after it had set.

It was an incredibly challenging season, and in its midst, I found many things to be angry at God for.

Just two years before I would find myself learning the ways of living with a colicky baby, I faced another difficult season. My oldest son was unexpectedly born two months prematurely and spent a month in the Neonatal Intensive Care Unit. Everett's premature birth was unexpected, abruptly ending my healthy pregnancy on December 13th, 2015. My water broke at 1:00 a.m., and I delivered my baby via emergency C-section at 3:53 that morning.

An Unexpected Entry into Motherhood

It was another difficult time for my husband and I. I spent every day at the NICU with my son, even though I could only hold him for an hour each day.

During that month in the hospital, my first month as a mom, I walked the sterile and lonely halls of the hospital, nearly always by myself. I ate alone in the cafeteria for lunch and spent endless hours in the provided room for NICU moms to pump.

Every two to three hours, I hooked myself up to a hospital-grade breast pump and watched as my milk dripped into a cup. The collected milk would then be handed to a nurse, who would feed it to my son through a tube.

This is not what I had hoped for in my first weeks as a mom. I was devastated. I spent my entire life dreaming of becoming a mom, and here I was, sitting alone most of my days, living for the short sixty minutes I could hold and touch my son.

I felt more like a visitor and onlooker rather than a mother during that time. As Everett laid warm in his incubator, I wished for him to be warm in my arms instead. I grieved for the baby that was not at my breast but instead fed through a tube in his nose.

As I rose at all hours of the night to hook myself to a breast pump in the bathroom at my father-in-law's house, where we stayed during that time, I sat on a cold toilet seat, tears slipping down my cheeks as the rhythmic woosh and thump of the pump was no match for the beating of my son's heart near mine.

My heart ached with a heaviness that was filled with the inability to hold and care for my son in the way I, even as a brand-new mom, knew instinctively to do. Every night that I left him until morning, exiting the doors of the NICU, riding down the cold and bumpy elevator and bracing for the harsh winter wind as I left the hospital, and my son behind, I felt filled with a helpless grief.

And yet, God was there.

Even through the unbearable pain and sorrow, His provision is clear. From the moment my water broke, even as terrifying as it was, we were all kept safe. Everett was born early but healthy, and he proved to be quite strong and is to this day. Family and friends stepped in to care for us in a multitude of ways, from taking care of our lodging for the month while we lived out of town to stay close to our son, to meals, financial support, bills, transportation, and more.

One evening near the middle of Everett's month-long NICU stay, I sat in my car alone, having left a grocery store in tears. The grief in my heart, the longing for my child, and the loneliness I felt as my husband and I both struggled through this difficult season, unsure of how to support one another while we both grieved and processed the trauma of the premature birth in our own ways. All of a sudden, it was too much, and I felt alone and helpless to bear it.

And then a gentle knock came to my window.

Startled at first, I then saw a woman with caring eyes and a gentle smile standing outside my car door. I cracked the window just enough to hear her ask if I was alright. She noticed me crying alone in my car and just wanted to check on me, she assured me. My answer was a simple yes but my eyes betrayed me, and I think she knew it was more complicated than that.

"May I pray for you?" she asked.

It was a hand reaching for me, pulling me from the sea of grief I felt helpless in. It was a freezing cold night so I only had her promise of prayers echoing in my ears as she gave me an encouraging nod and hopped into her car. As we drove our separate ways, I felt the heartache ease and the presence of peace wash away a little of the grief. That night, God met me in the parking lot of a grocery store, using the kindness of a stranger to remind me that I wasn't alone and that His peace transcends all earthly obstacles that stand against it.

Another Test of Faith

A few years later, my husband and I were ecstatic that I had made it full term with our second baby boy. It seemed we had been cleared for a much easier ride this time.

In the weeks following Jack's trauma-free birth, he began to show signs of colic, characterized by prolonged, intense crying and fussiness.

I was confident that the colic would soon pass simply because Google said so.

But it did not.

And with every day of unending crying and screaming that we endured, my faith also took a beating.

I was angry with the complications and challenges that motherhood had brought me again, this time with my second son, and I pointed my resentment at the Lord in my weakest moments.

Nearly two and a half years later, we received the official diagnosis from the geneticist that would confirm what we already knew: Jack has a rare chromosomal deletion called William's Syndrome.

It was a day I'll never forget. One filled with the warmth and sunshine of early summer. The lupin and yellow wildflowers were entirely in bloom, like a blanket of color upon the hill outside our backdoor.

We had known about this rare genetic syndrome since my birthday back in February of that year, about three and a half months before his official diagnosis.

During that interim period of knowing in our hearts what was true and waiting for the formality of an official diagnosis, I had begun my grieving process.

While it felt like holding my breath as we waited for that day in June to arrive, once it was upon us, and we had the confirmation staring us in the face in black ink printed on white paper, I felt like I could finally breathe again.

Somehow, amid the overlapping feelings of grief and joy, a bridge had been built, connecting my grief to the other side, to a place where I could finally feel relief.

We finally had the answers to why Jack had been so colicky, had feeding issues, sleeping difficulties, missed milestones, and more. So many puzzle pieces clicked into place, giving us a surprising but clearer picture of who Jack is and why we had faced such struggles with him as a baby.

As I walked out of our house and into the late afternoon sunshine, finding Jack playing on the patio with his brother, I took him in my arms, joy filling the spaces within me that had once been hollowed out by grief.

As I walked out of our house and into the late afternoon sunshine, finding Jack playing on the patio with his brother, I took him in my arms, joy filling the spaces within me that had once been hollowed out by grief.

I took a selfie of the two of us to remember that day and that moment—our genuine smiles as the sun bathed us in a golden glow. The two of us looked so happy and free.

In those moments when I was angry with God, I felt at the center of a raging storm and even became a storm myself. Enraged by my difficult circumstances, feeling robbed of what I felt entitled to have, I had the biggest questions I've ever had as a believer burning within me.

Why was God choosing this path for my life? Why was He allowing me to struggle so much? Why was my motherhood journey—one of the deepest desires of my heart—coming with such a steep and rocky climb?

I wasn't enjoying motherhood during the first year Jack was born. It was painfully difficult, and I couldn't make sense of why God would allow it, especially after how much I struggled after Everett was born so early.

Thinking back on my anger during that time, I can't help but think of Job.

Job, a righteous man before God, lost everything of value and nearly everyone he loved; even his health suffered greatly. In the book of Job, we see that God allowed him to be tested by Satan, and in his great suffering, he cried out to God.

"Therefore, I will not restrain my mouth; I will speak in the anguish of my spirit, I will complain in the bitterness of my soul" (Job 7:11).

Doubting God's faithfulness doesn't make us unbelievers; it just means we are human.

When my faith is slipping, I can't help but remember the disciples in a boat tossed at sea. Upon seeing Jesus walking on water toward them, His disciple Peter got out of the boat and miraculously walked on the water, too.

And Peter answered Him and said, "Lord, if it is You, command me to come to You on the water." So He said, "Come." And when Peter had come down out of the boat, he walked on the water to go to Jesus. But when he saw that the wind was boisterous, he was afraid; and beginning to sink he cried out, saying, "Lord, save me!" And immediately Jesus stretched out His hand and caught him, and said to him, "O you of little faith, why did you doubt?" (Matthew 14:28-31)

Peter started out bold and full of faith, but as his eyes drifted from Jesus, and he remembered the storm around him, he began to sink.

How often do we lose sight of Jesus and notice the storm raging around us instead of our Savior?

I'm often keenly aware of the whip of winds, the slap of rain upon my face, the pounding thunder as it rages within the sky above me, and the crushing depth of endless sea just inches below as I am tossed amidst the storms of my life.

All of this drives me to anger, fear, frustration, and doubt.

But how aware am I of the presence of Jesus and His outstretched arm, waiting for me to grab hold and be rescued to peace?

In keeping my eyes on Him and my hand in His, He offers me a walk upon the water.

He beckons me toward a faith that looms larger than my fears, a faith that casts fear into the stormy depths of the raging sea until there is nothing left of rage and storm. There is only peace.

And a faith that propels me out of the boat.

Amazing Grace

It's hard to admit when our faith is under fire, and we can feel the flames lick away at what we thought to be fireproof in our lives.

While my heart and mind both know that God is all of my hope, joy, and peace, my deceitful heart will still forget His goodness. Instead of clinging to Him, I'll flee toward my own selfish and wicked ways, fanning the flames of my anger and rage or drowning in the sea of my own pity.

That's unsettling to admit, as well.

And yet, no matter my mood over life's unfairness, God is not pushed away. In fact, it's just me who storms off and slams the door. He is immovable in His love for me, no matter my tantrums.

As parents, we should get that pretty well. No tantrum my child threw ever stopped me from loving them.

This journey is challenging, and it might feel as though you are stumbling down your path rather than walking. But here's what you can do to find some sturdier steps and keep moving in the right direction.

Pray. Pray over all of your big emotions and ask God to give you peace in place of them. Pray before you begin your day, during the middle of your day, and at the end of your day. Think of them like little gas stations along the journey of your day, fueling you up for what lies ahead.

Create a routine that keeps you in a close relationship with God. All relationships flourish when we are daily involved with one another, and your relationship with God is no different. Think of your relationship like a muscle. Your muscles don't go away if you don't exercise, but they get much stronger and more noticeable if you do. The same is true of our faith; if you want to have a strong, notable faith, work on it daily.

Remember this formula whenever you need a heart change: prayer + praise = peace. I don't always feel like praying or turning on some worship music, but I'm always grateful when I do. Inviting God into my heart through prayer and praise is a perfect recipe to bring about peace. It doesn't mean the mountains are going to move, but your heart sure will.

My friend, I'm so glad we are on this journey together. We may have come by it unexpectedly, but I have no doubt it was orchestrated for a reason. We might struggle with doubts or experience anger and frustration, but I'm so glad our God is unsurprised by our doubts and struggles. I'm so grateful He gets us, loving us through all the awkward, regrettable parts of our journeys.

I'm so grateful for His amazing, amazing grace.

Reflect and Pray

"Come to Me, all you who labor and are heavy laden, and I will give you rest. Take My yoke upon you and learn from Me, for I am gentle and lowly in heart, and you will find rest for your souls. For My yoke is easy and My burden is light" (Matthew 11:28-30).

What Jesus offers us here is freedom from the burdens we carry in life. Not that all responsibilities cease to exist but that through Him, we can find rest from the weariness of this world.

Remember the fruits of the Spirit? Love, joy, peace, patience, kindness, goodness, faithfulness, gentleness, and self-control are the fruits of the Spirit. Imagine how each of those things would change the way we handle the burdens that we bear.

And if you feel that your faith is feeling fragile today, pray over it now.

1.   In what ways has it been difficult for me to stay faithful after receiving the diagnosis for my child? What emotions have I felt?

2.   How has my faith grown since receiving the diagnosis?

A Prayer for the Mom Whose Faith is Under Fire

Heavenly Father, I come to You with a heart heavy with doubt and confusion. My faith feels weak, and I am struggling to hold on to the assurance of Your presence and love.

Help me to remember Your promises and to trust in Your plans, even when I cannot see the way forward. Fill me with Your peace that surpasses all understanding, and strengthen my faith as I navigate through these challenges.

Lord, remind me of Your unending grace and mercy. Help me to lean on Your word and to seek You in prayer, knowing that You are always near, even when I feel distant.

Thank you for Your patience with me. Renew my spirit and help me to find joy and hope in Your unfailing love. Surround me with Your light and let it guide me back to a place of trust and faith in You.

In the precious and holy name of Jesus, Amen.

CHAPTER SIX

Walking in Faithfulness

We once lived in a house with a long, gravel driveway. Nestled within fields that had once been farmed stood a two-story farmhouse we called home for a while.

During the school year, I often pushed a stroller up and down our long driveway as my daughter and I walked to meet the school bus her older brothers rode on.

One day in the late spring, we left for the afternoon bus a bit earlier than usual. It was the kind of spring day you long for when winter is harsh, when everything is dead and frozen, and you cannot wait to fill your eyes with scenes of green grass and trees bursting with soft petals, while hearing the serenade of birds filling the air with song.

It was during this afternoon walk as my daughter and I strolled up and down the driveway, relishing in the sun's warmth, the light breeze that tickled strands of hair from behind our ears, and the distinctly beautiful melody of the meadowlark, that I spotted something unexpected on our path.

Bending over to examine what I thought was a broken piece of glass was instead the unmistakable translucence of an amber-colored agate, a rock common to where I live that can range in size and color. The agates I often find are either smooth and round or dimpled with lumps and bumps, and they vary in color from yellow to orange to red.A newfound hobby was born for me as I held the small agate to the sun and watched it glow.

For months after that day, I paced up and down our driveway, often bent over at the waist, inspecting the rocks beneath me and hoping for a familiar glimmer to catch my eye.

I collected the small agates I found into a tall mason jar, filling it about one-quarter full when summer ended. The agates were mainly the size of a pencil eraser, but some were as big as a quarter. I proudly displayed my agate collection in the kitchen window for all to see.

As the agate-collecting continued, I began to find fewer and fewer. Oddly enough, I never ventured from where I first saw them, always assuming my success was within the borders of our driveway.

Later in the fall, while walking through the fields surrounding our house with my children, I stumbled upon a much larger agate, about half the size of my palm, tucked into the soil beneath my feet. You can imagine my astonishment. In all my agate-hunting along the driveway, agates larger than I had ever seen were but a few feet away.

Over the next several weeks, until winter came and laid a blanket of snow upon the earth, I filled my pockets with agates of every shape, size, and color. Soon, I filled the mason jar and started a second jar with agates ranging from the size of my thumb to the palm of my hand. The farther out I ventured, and the more steps I took within the rocky patches that slithered through the open, grassy fields, the more of my treasure I would find.

One afternoon, while my daughter was inside for a nap and my husband was home, I slipped out for a solo agate hunt. Walking the fields meant an opportunity for prayer and conversation with God, as had become my habit. My mind and heart have always felt most open to the Lord when I am alone outdoors, imagining He is walking beside me as a friend.

I found so many agates that day. As I filled my pocket and continued in my prayer and quiet conversation with God, I then asked Him to show me an agate more giant than I'd yet to see. The wind seemed to billow in my face and dance through my hair in answer. I assumed that was a yes from God, so I kept searching.

But the largest agate I'd ever found was not there.

I eventually walked home and then toward the chicken pen, where my husband and sons were. As we stood beside our busy hens, watching them peck at the grass beneath them, my oldest suddenly bent over to scoop something up. As he stood, Everett held up the largest agate I'd ever seen with a smile that reached his ears. It had been there all along, near the barnyard, right next to the chickens. I wondered how many days I'd walked right by it and not noticed it.

We all laughed out loud and admired the treasure that I had been obsessing over for a while. Later that day, I added it to my collection, still in amazement at God's craftiness and meticulous attention to detail. He truly works in fun and mysterious ways, always knowing how to bring a smile to our faces.

Walking in faithfulness means trusting that He has bigger and better plans for us beyond the limits of our comprehension and imagination. Even when we feel defeated by a diagnosis or the limitations we see our child struggle with, walking faithfully with the Lord throughout this journey means recognizing our need for Him in all aspects of this parenting role and our lives. Like my dainty, little driveway agates compared to the massive and abundant agates from the surrounding fields, I have to recognize that what I am capable of on my own is nothing compared to what God can equip me for.

Those moments spent scouting the driveway for agates were moments of peace for me. They granted me an opportunity to clear my head and heart after long, hard days, anxieties about specialist appointments, Individualized Eduation Progam (IEP) meetings, fears for the future, or any current struggle waiting for me as soon as I walked back in the door at home.

But what I could find on my own, God could multiply.

Just like He showed me the abundance of agates outside my once-limited hunting ground, He offers me more than I can ever find on my own. Some of my greatest needs are peace, strength, rest, joy, and grace, as well as to be loved and seen for who I am, especially in this unique role. There is no greater source for all of those things than God.

Self-Care that Sustains

As special needs moms we know that rest is crucial and unfortunately, hard to come by. We often feel burnt out and weary, sometimes lacking in the support we need to give ourselves a much needed break. We might struggle for peace, be desperate for strength and rest, find it hard to feel joy, needing grace, and to be loved and seen for all that I do, feel, and bear daily. We might feel painfully invisible to others and afraid or unable to ask for help.

Self-care is often seen as a luxury for a mom raising a child with special needs, but in reality, it is essential for sustaining both spiritual and physical well-being. As moms, we are called to pour into our families with love, patience, and strength, but that can only happen when we are also filling our own cup. For the Christian mom, self-care isn't just about spa days or getting a break—it's about taking intentional time to rest in the presence of God. Jesus himself modeled the importance of retreating to be with the Father (Mark 1:35), reminding us that true refreshment is found in the One who offers living water. Incorporating practices like prayer, meditation on scripture, and even simply taking moments to breathe deeply and focus on God's promises can be a powerful way to renew your spirit amidst the demands of caring for a child with special needs.

Battling the daily challenges we face, navigating the complex medical and educational needs, managing other children and our marriages, and dealing with the ever-rising tide of fear and anxiety that preys upon our hearts and minds, we certainly need something more than temporary rest to soothe our weary souls.

Self-care also means recognizing that your value does not come from how much you accomplish but from who you are in Christ. It's easy to get lost in the constant demands of caregiving, but you are more than just the tasks you complete. God's grace is sufficient for you, even on days when everything feels overwhelming (2 Corinthians 12:9). Embracing rest, seeking support from family, friends, or community, and prioritizing your own mental and emotional health can be acts of faith—acknowledging that God's strength is made perfect in your weakness. In caring for yourself, you are better equipped to care for your family and reflect God's love to them. Remember that you are a beloved daughter of the King, and He desires for you to experience His peace and joy, even in the midst of the challenges.

If you're like me, you look forward to opportunities for personal hobbies and interests, outside of being a mom. However difficult it can be to pursue such things during certain seasons of motherhood, we know that God designed each of us with unique interests, talents, and passions, and He delights in seeing us enjoy them.

For moms, especially those who carry the weight of caring for a child with special needs, engaging in hobbies isn't just about taking a break—it's an opportunity to experience joy and creativity, gifts that come from God. Ecclesiastes 3:13 reminds us that "every man should eat and drink and enjoy the good of all his labor—it is the gift of God." This includes finding joy in the simple pleasures in life. Whether it's crafting, reading, gardening, or any other interest, pursuing hobbies allows moms to reconnect with the joy and fulfillment that God intends for His children. These moments of enjoyment can refresh your spirit and remind you that you are not defined solely by your roles and responsibilities. Embracing your hobbies is a way of acknowledging that God cares not just about your duties, but about your joy and well-being, too.

In this season of life, I may not be able to chase all of my passions, but I'm grateful for the fields I can wander, the agates I can gather in my pockets, and the way I can invite the Lord into this simple joy. The fresh air, exercise, solitude, and time with God refresh and strengthen my heart and soul.

Life-giving hobbies and modes of self-care will look different for each of us, but we must also pursue a daily walk with Jesus so that we are never without the encouragement, strength, and hope His presence offers us.

He Sees and Meets Our Needs

Early one summer, my entire family was sick. It was a dreadful combination of the flu and a respiratory virus.

As each of my three children came down with this awful sickness, my husband and I stayed healthy and took shifts for a couple of nights caring for the kids as they each took turns waking up in the middle of the night not feeling well and needing the bathroom, some water, some more medicine, or just the soothing touch of Mom or Dad.

I was exhausted within nearly a week of this routine, but then my husband went down, and I was the last one standing. Feeling tired to my bones and knowing that I was in for another night of little sleep and likely going to be sick next, I felt panic rising in my chest throughout the day.

"Lord, help me get through this," I prayed as I went about the day, cleaning up vomit and washing bed sheets and towels.

As I tucked my kids into their beds and my husband on the couch, I felt an internal tug on my heart that said, "Meet Me outside."

Knowing that God was speaking to me, I obliged as soon as possible. By early evening, in the sunset glow of early summer, I slipped on a pair of sandals and walked outside for the first time in days. I could have laid down right there in the cool grass of our lawn for an hour, but I felt the pull to head out a bit farther.

The area where we lived at that time was surrounded by fields that were once farmland. Old wheat fields were now giving life to baby pine trees sprouting throughout the tall, wispy grasses that reached the tops of my thighs.

As I walked toward a line of old, tall pine trees, I felt the exhaustion and weight of the last days within my chest. Like a pair of shoelaces you might unknot after a long run, I could feel the tension easing and pulling, about to break free into a monumental sob.

Did God call me out here to have a good cry? If so, I was ready for it. The hot tears were near stinging my eyes, and the tangled emotions fought to burst forth as I walked on, grass catching between my toes as my sandals held to my feet.

I would burst into tears at any moment. And I sure do love a good cry.

But then something incredible happened.

The bright honey-colored sunset light burst through an opening in the trees and immediately halted my tracks. All at once, I took in the cascading glow it bathed the world around me in.

Pine needles shone as if dusted by sunset glitter, and the field looked washed in bronze, glowing all around me. I noticed a butterfly gracefully dancing by, and then there was the hum and buzz of a few other insects as they bobbed in front of me.

It was as if all living things, from each blade of grass to the top of every tree, from a butterfly's grace to a bee's buzz, were shining in the light of God's glory and responding in worship to Him.

At that exact moment, I took all of this in and was filled with the most incredible peace I'd ever experienced. It surpassed all my understanding, just like the scripture said it would (Philippians 4:7).

God knows exactly what we are going through, just as well as He knows our greatest needs. And unlike anything else this world can offer, He can meet those needs in the most unexpected and beautiful ways.

Walking in faithfulness with God means spending time with Him so that we can hear His voice, discern His truth, and feel His presence daily.

And it often is like stepping outside of what we know to follow something we can't yet see. Much like my beloved agate hunts, I initially had such limited vision while hunting, and it kept me from finding the bountiful treasure that awaited me. When I realized that our driveway was a small sampling of the agates in the area, I couldn't believe I had never thought to look elsewhere. It suddenly didn't make any sense to stay in the same area, even though I had spent weeks doing the same thing repeatedly without thinking of lifting my head to look beyond my limited scope.

God's vision is far greater, more advanced, and more knowledgeable than we could imagine. God exists outside space and time, while we are intrinsically limited to them. How dare we ever imagine we know better than He. When I think of it like that, I'm baffled at my ego, yet I do it all the time, this inability to let go and let God, as they say.

Like Sarah from the Old Testament, I often cannot see how God will make something happen, so I take matters into my own hands. Or I doubt His ways, timing, or promises, so I keep my eyes down, scanning my small, picked-over path for something I'll never find.

The Truth of Walking in Faithfulness

In my early season as a special needs mom, after being devastated by the diagnosis, I seemed to be on a roller coaster of grief. One day, I felt the bliss of climbing high toward the sky, with the sun on my face as I motored toward heaven, only to experience the gut-blasting plunge back toward earth the next day.

I had never experienced grief like this before, one that changes so quickly and without notice. It often reminds me of how the tide changes when I visit the beach. I've stood barefoot in the sand, waiting for the water to gently kiss my toes and softly glide over my feet while listening to the calls and cries of seagulls. Other times, I've witnessed the crash and tumble of waves and ran as they chased me with a fierceness and a roar that drowned out any other noise.

Walking in faithfulness doesn't mean there won't ever be an angry sea that chases me away from the peace of a gentle surge of water tickling my ankles, but it does mean I can have peace, regardless of how loudly my grief roars.

When we walk with God, we can be sure that He has bigger things in store for us, so we can step outside the comforts of what we know and follow Him.

We can learn to hear His voice and experience the unimaginable peace and strength only He can give us.

We can handle whatever the day brings and bravely walk into any medical appointment or an IEP meeting at school, knowing He is with us and goes before us.

We can learn, and relearn, how to parent our special needs child, can give and receive grace for all the difficulties we go through and all the times we don't show up the way we want to, all because He is with us.

He is with us and faithful to us, entirely suitable for guiding us along our path and equipping us for the role He chose us for.

We Walk by Faith, Not Sight

The journey looms before you, and I know you're struggling with what might lie ahead, waiting for you. I've been there, too—precisely in that same spot. So many unknowns darken your skies like thunderclouds rolling in.

But it doesn't have to feel that way.

"Your word is a lamp to my feet and a light to my path" (Psalm 119:105).

God's Word guides us, providing direction, clarity, wisdom, and truth to navigate through our journeys and the challenges in our paths. We are so much better with Him than away from Him, my friend.

When I think of us as newly appointed special needs moms, I think of the Israelites, fresh from Egypt and the only life they ever knew. As they began their new life, wandering through the desert on their way to the Promised Land, God led them with light. Night or day, He led them with light.

"And the Lord went before them by day in a pillar of cloud to lead them along the way, and by night in a pillar of fire to give them light, that they might travel by day and by night" (Exodus 13:21, ESV).

We travel day and night, too, don't we? We constantly maneuver our way along this journey with our child. We will always need the light of help. Thankfully, God is always with us, and His light is always illuminating our steps.

"And the Lord, He is the One who goes before you. He will be with you, He will not leave you nor forsake you; do not fear nor be dismayed" (Deuteronomy 31:8).

When we walk by faith, we take steps toward and with God. Walking in faith is an act of submission, and we must recognize our need for Him and create space for Him in our daily lives. We spend time in scripture, pray, worship, and fellowship with other believers: in doing these things, our faith is strengthened. A strong faith is precisely what we need to take us on the road ahead.

If this routine feels daunting, start with 5-10 minutes daily, breaking it up if necessary—five minutes of prayers and five minutes of reading scripture or a daily devotional. God meets you where you are, not where you think you should be.

The truth about walking is that the more you walk, the stronger you get, the farther you can go, and the more scenery you can take in. The more you walk with the Lord daily, the stronger your faith, the more sustained you will be, and the more beauty and blessings you will encounter.

So grab your walking shoes and go—Jesus is right there on the path with you.

Reflect and Pray

Amid a difficult season of my own, someone asked me how I was able to stay so positive and faithful. It was a question but I took it as a compliment, as I realized that this outwardly obvious faithfulness was a product of my spiritual growth and daily walk with Jesus.

This had not always been the case but like a muscle that grows in size with consistent use, my own walk with the Lord was becoming more obvious to others as I had begun to show up consistently in my relationship with Him.

Walking in faithfulness is about building a relationship with God, but it's also about living in obedience to Him. We can see from the stories of Moses, Mary the mother of Jesus, and the twelve disciples how God worked through their obedience to accomplish incredible things. And we can be assured that our heavenly Father has incredible things in mind for us as well.

1.   How can you begin to walk in faithfulness? Or, how can you better walk in faithfulness?

2.   How can you begin to live a life of obedience to God? What might that look like for you in the season you are currently in?

3.   Do you have a daily routine for spending time with God? If not, how can you begin to incorporate one?

A Prayer for the Mom Who Walks in Faithfulness

Heavenly Father, I thank you for the relationship I can have with You. I am so grateful for the ability to walk with You daily and learn from Your word how to grow spiritually.

Thank you for working in my heart to transform me, and I ask that You continue to grow and strengthen me for all that You have planned for me in this life.

I ask that You will help me to lead a Spirit-led life so that I point others to You, and I teach my children about You throughout everyday life. I pray that in all that I do, I will honor and glorify You.

I pray that in this role as a special needs mom, You will guide me in walking faithfully through each part of this unique journey, as it includes a variety of ways I will need to advocate for my child, whether it be for medical needs or concerns, school needs or concerns, or anything else that my child will need. Help me to walk in faithfulness as I raise, advocate for, and love my child.

Lord, help me to find moments of rest and renewal in Your presence. When I feel weary, refresh my spirit and grant me the energy I need to continue the journey. Strengthen my resolve to live according to Your word, and guide my steps with Your wisdom.

In the precious and holy name of Jesus, Amen.

CHAPTER SEVEN

An Unexpected Community

The term "special needs mom" felt as if it was sinking in for me within the first year of the diagnosis, passing through the barrier of my skin and into my bones, my heart, and my soul.

But it still didn't feel real.

How could I become something I had never considered an option? How could I walk a path I never imagined my feet to fall upon?

And while my son Jack was still very young at that time, my mind kept lurching forward to an unknown future. What would our lives be like twenty years from now, caring for our adult son and never expecting him to leave home, like other grown children often do? I wondered. Isolated by the prison of my thoughts, I worried endlessly about the future that might lie before us due to his diagnosis.

My son was an incredible gift, yet I could not help but worry that we would never be able to watch him spread his wings and fly—or at least not in the way we had expected, not in the way I still longed for. And in those moments, I felt my heart rip in two, one side pitted against the other: a part of me brimming with gratitude and the other seething with bitterness.

Looking around at my closest friends and family, I saw that no one was like me in this regard.

Like a memory of something yet to happen, I could feel the heaviness of my heart as I imagined myself someday sitting with a group of friends as they, one by one, listed the incredible accomplishments and milestones their grown kids were experiencing out in the world. And while I would always be proud of my son and all he would do, I felt sad about what we would inevitably miss out on for him.

Yes, my new role of special needs mom was sinking in, coating everything within me with the weight of isolation. My heart, heaviest of all, as I began to feel those first feelings of loneliness. Like a heavy but invisible coat I couldn't get off, those feelings were cloaking me in isolation.

Perhaps you know this feeling just as well. While we might not truly be alone with our kids, families, and friends always around, we often feel like we've been dropped onto a deserted island, even amid a sea of loved ones.

Before I shared my son's diagnosis with more than close family and friends, and before I tapped "share" on that first public Instagram post—sharing with the world my son's diagnosis—I was searching for others like me. Those I might find on the same journey I now found myself on. And because of the Internet, it took mere seconds to locate others.

And while there are certainly plenty of things to dislike about the Internet and social media these days, we can also find lots to be grateful for because of it. Such as hashtags and support groups that instantly connect us with what we seek.

After searching for my son's diagnosis as a hashtag, I was immediately face to face with moms just like me, their feeds lit up with the glow of a smile I knew well with its broadness, spaced-apart teeth, and the little, upturned nose that sat above it. And with a vulnerability that felt like a bit of a band-aid administered to help heal my raw and gaping wound, their posts and stories greeted me like a soothing balm.

I was drawn in by these women's joys, victories, defeats, and losses. From the devastation of the diagnosis to the beauty-from-ashes stories that unfolded, I discovered a triumphant truth.

I was not alone.

Tears fell as I immediately connected with Internet strangers I would never meet. Just like shedding an unnecessary jacket on a warm spring day, I realized I didn't need to stay cloaked in loneliness and isolation.

There they were, parents from all parts of the country and the world, with different backgrounds and native languages, bonded together by something entirely rare that leveled the playing field for us all.

We were all united by one distinct commonality: the William's Syndrome diagnosis of our child. And because of that unique diagnosis, we could easily relate to one another, regardless of nationality, language, or location.

Conversations centered around how we were coping, what struggle we were currently up against, IEP meetings, and cardiology appointments, all incredibly unique to our child's exact diagnosis. With an ease that refreshed me, conversations came quickly and easily within this group, as if the need for the typical time and introductions of most friendships was swept away, and a distinct camaraderie was ushered in, granting us all the ability to share our hearts in a much-needed way.

For one friend in particular, messages turned into voice memos, and it didn't even matter that we were living completely different lives in different countries, half a world away from one another. We each have a boy with William's Syndrome, and for that knowledge alone, we have a lifetime of conversation to bounce back and forth upon moving forward.

As her life unfolded before mine via Instagram stories and posts, I could see so much of my son in hers. As our boys are a few years apart, her son younger than mine, I witnessed a similar journey she was embarking on that I knew well. What a joy and a privilege to know her and share something so unique, special, and rare that its mere presence has linked us in this life.

What a gift she is to me, and these friendships online are to us all.

The friendships that don't need the traditional ingredients but are born out of a common denominator—a shared diagnosis, a similar story, and footsteps along a shared path.

I imagine it like this: We are all trudging along the same path, feeling incredibly alone and isolated, but we get the sense that others are walking alongside us. We might hear their voices or notice the tread of a shoe marked along the path before us. We sometimes hear weeping, and our cheeks drip with tears in response, crying softly for a shared pain no words require. Other times, we hear laughter and smile, glad to know others are finding joy along the way since we, too, are finding joy along this journey.

Suddenly, while we tread on, somehow unaware of the many others walking beside us, we are no longer invisible to one another. But there, beside us, in front and behind us, are parents and their children, walking this same path. The sound of their footsteps is like an unbroken chorus that weeps and shouts with the mingling of joy and sorrow: You are not alone!

And that, my friend, is what the Internet does for us.

Not long after I received the diagnosis for my son, I was greeted by a fellow special needs mom of 20+ years who expressed to me that she wished she'd had the Internet when she was going through those early years post-diagnosis.

And I felt for her because the Internet, with so many reasons to complain or be wary of it, was helping me find my people, granting me answers, ideas, and suggestions for what to try or research next as I began to understand, advocate for, and raise my son.

The diagnosis and the community it has brought with it were unexpected, but the gratitude that they came hand in hand with it is undeniable.

A Community of Connection and Support

This unexpected community reminds me of the disciples and the unexpected crew that they were. They were a rag-tag bunch, from fishermen to tax collectors, doubters, warriors, and sinners—not at all who you might link together if you were thinking of who should follow and represent the Messiah.

But God has always been more concerned with our hearts: regardless of their pasts, struggles, predispositions, or sins, their hearts were the ones for the job.

Looking at the disciples this way, we can be confident that God calls us all to follow the route He has set before us. We are all here on this journey, walking alongside one another for a purpose greater than ourselves, and we, too, just might have been hand-selected for the task because of our hearts.

Admittedly, I sometimes think of what life would be like if I didn't carry this "special needs mom" title, and my neurodivergent son had been born neurotypical instead. Would life be a bit easier?

But the longer I walk this road, the more I realize God selected me to steward this task, and in my submission to this calling, I am giving Him glory. I may feel unqualified for the role some days, but God knows what I do not, including what I am truly capable of. The disciples must have felt the same way as they took on these entirely new and unforeseen roles from Jesus. And how difficult it would have been for them to do it alone. But instead, with the grace and goodness of God, He planned for them to all be together, united by something others would never understand.

Those unqualified, undeniably different men, the disciples of Jesus, are profoundly beautiful specimens of God's love, understanding, and compassion for us. And while He calls us to a greater task, we aren't called to do it alone, for He has a pattern of creating community. Scripture gives several examples of when God brought in a helper for His children.

Adam had Eve.

Moses had Aaron.

Naomi had Ruth.

Mary, the mother of Jesus, had Elizabeth.

The twelve disciples had each other.

Our heavenly Father knows the desires and needs of our hearts, and while He knows we need Him most of all, He also understands our need for one another. As our Creator, He is intimately aware of the good it makes our weary hearts feel when we connect with others who have traveled or are traveling along the same path. How good it is when we walk alongside a friend with our shared joys, victories, and sorrows, knowing because they are there, we are set free from isolation and unbound from loneliness. Like a helping hand along the same steep and rocky path, we can cheer and encourage one another onward toward those mountain views we all get to enjoy on this extraordinary journey.

Therefore, while I unexpectedly find myself on a path that few have traveled, with God's great love and divine attention to detail, I rarely walk alone. Whether it be Facebook groups, Instagram hashtags, or the friends I have made through them, I am always just a post, a message, or a voice memo away from a friend who gets me in a way not all others do. In this day and age, it might as well be like tapping the shoulder next to me as we soldier on the journey ahead of us both.

It's an unexpected community God lovingly designed, prepared, and expected for us all along.

You are Not Alone

I had never heard of William's Syndrome before.

And while I know others who have children with disabilities, I had never imagined it would become a part of my life, too.

Until one day, it became very much a part of my life.

For months after my son's diagnosis, it felt as if I was waking disoriented from a dream, and each morning, I was remembering the diagnosis all over again. And while my life felt abruptly halted by it all, everyone else's life continued on. It was a lonely time, carrying the weight of fresh grief while also appearing as if I was carrying nothing at all. Many others seemed to have moved on from what I could not break free from. A grief that halted my steps and altered my entire life felt tragically unseen and forgotten by others.

I wanted to be strong, to have it all figured out, to be on the other side of grief, and, most of all, to get back to living life the way everyone else was, the way I once had. But getting to the other side of anything takes just one step at a time.

So there I was, taking what felt like baby steps when I found a community ofspecial needs parents and William's Syndrome parents online, which changed my world. Instead of feeling alone with my grief and fears, I was surrounded by other parents who had walked this same path, carrying the heavy weight of their grief and fears once, too.

As if they had passed me a torch to shed light on this new path I was stumbling around on, their words were like a remedy to the aches and pains of my heart.

It will be okay. It will get easier. I felt that way once, too.

And they were right. It is okay; it did get easier. And by the way, I'm handing you a torch now, too, my fellow readers. Shine it around and see that this new world is pretty amazing, and plenty of us are here with you.

Remember that you are not alone in any of it—in your grief, the worries that keep you up at night, or the anxious thoughts for the future. There is a community here, ready to be tapped on the shoulder when you need us to help.

Reflect and Pray

The Bible is full of examples on how to have a right relationship with God, but it's also packed with what to do and what not to do in relationship with others.

Friendship is a theme we see often throughout scripture. And one of my favorite friendship duos is Naomi and Ruth. Their love and devotion to one another, through heartache and loss, transcends time and culture. It's a beautiful depiction of sticking by someone's side, through thick and thin.

Naomi, a widow, has two sons, and one of them marries Ruth. But then Ruth's husband dies, so Naomi urges her newly widowed daughter-in-law to returnto her own land and people, which would have been customary back then. But in a sweet twist of events, Ruth chooses Naomi over going back home. She says, "Wherever you go, I will go; and wherever you lodge, I will lodge; your people shall be my people, and your God, my God" (Ruth 1:16).

Ruth sticks by Naomi's side, and eventually she remarries and has a son. Through her lineage, Jesus would eventually be born, as well.

Can you imagine the delight Naomi must have had when, after losing her own husband and sons, her daughter-in-law sticks by her side, remarries, and bears children she would help raise? Both of them, through their devotion to one another, were given another chance at happiness.

Sometimes true friendships come from the most unlikely places. Often in our journey, we will feel alone, isolated from even our closest friends and family because they don't understand our struggle. In what ways is God bringing unexpected friendships into your life? Pray over your current and future friendships and trust that God is sending you exactly who you need in your life.

1. In what ways have you struggled with friendships since receiving the diagnosis for your child?

2. In what ways have some friendships gotten stronger since receiving the diagnosis for your child?

3. What are some ways that you can allow yourself to seek new or different friendships in this new season?

A Prayer for the Mom Seeking Her People

Heavenly Father, I sometimes feel totally alone in this journey as a special needs mom, feeling alone in my struggles and jealous of others who seem to have it easier than I do. I ask for freedom from both of these feelings and that you would build in me a heart of gratitude and contentedness.

Lord, You created us to live in fellowship with one another, and You know the deep need we have for connection and encouragement. I ask that You bring people into my life who will walk alongside me, sharing the burdens and celebrating the joys.

Father, grant me the courage to reach out and seek the support I often need. Help me to find groups, friends, and communities where I feel welcomed and understood.

I ask for opportunities for meaningful connections and divine appointments that will bring the right people into my life at the right time.

Help me to also be a source of support and encouragement to others, creating a network of love and care.
Lord, may Your love flow through these friendships and communities, making them places of refuge, strength, and joy. Help us grow in faith and resiliency through the support of others and always feel Your presence in the midst of our journey.

Father God, I pray over the community in my life, made up of friends and family who love me and my child. I thank you for them.

In the precious and holy name of Jesus, Amen.

CHAPTER EIGHT

Conquering the Mountains That Don't Move

The sun's relentless heat bears down upon you, and a cloudless blue sky doesn't show the promise of escape from its blazing rays. The task set before you feels even more daunting as you stand there, sweating in the sun.

You've paced around but haven't moved beyond your starting point. Even though you've yet to progress in your ascent, your legs feel as heavy as tree trunks, and the pit in your stomach feels like lead.

Looking up, you can see a steep, winding path. Seeing it causes your mouth to dry out and a cold sweat to emerge on your skin, even though the sun still bears down on you.

You're at the base of a mountain and have yet to climb.

With its steep, rocky terrain, unending challenges, and unprecedented obstacles, this mountain is yours, and you must climb it.

You feel profoundly unqualified, and fear washes over you like the sweat dripping down your face and back. There must be some mistake.

Dropping to your knees in prayer, knowing God can move mountains, you squint your eyes and earnestly ask for a miracle.

Opening your eyes, you see the mountain continues to loom overhead. It really is yours to climb.

Just as you begin to feel faint from the heat and the hike ahead, a cool breeze whispers by, and a cloud you didn't notice before begins to block the sun, giving you a respite from the scorching heat.

Basking in the instant coolness, you look up at your mountain and see something you didn't see before.

The most beautiful wildflowers litter the path to the top, and while it is pretty steep, there are little benches carved into the mountain, bursting with lush green trees and grasses that offer comfort and rest for your journey. A waterfall playfully splashes near the peak, and you suddenly notice the featherlight kiss of a water droplet that has pirouetted down to your cheeks.

With shaky, uncertain steps, you begin your ascent, equally terrified and curious about the journey ahead. But as you start your climb, the scent of wildflowers, the softness of the grass, the generous shade of the trees, and the unparalleled views you imagine you'll find along the way propel you forward.

An Unexpected Climb

I often think of my experience as a special needs mom like climbing a mountain. It sure is daunting when I gaze up at the mountain, and during my trek, I am faced with regular challenges that make it one of the hardest climbs I have ever taken.

But then there is the joy we find in this journey—a truly remarkable joy like the glistening water we see from the surface, in the form of the unparalleled compassion and joy our special kiddos exhibit, so quickly and uninhibited than the rest of us are capable of. Or it's like the wonders deep within the ocean waters, like the hard-won milestones and skills our children work diligently for, most of which are seen only by those willing to take on that deep dive of a journey.

As parents, we are familiar with playing the long game with our children. How often do we hold their tiny hands while helping them practice walking on wobbly feet before they gain the ability and confidence to take those first steps of independence? How many hours would it be if we totaled the sum of all the times we helped our children get dressed, lace up their shoes, brush their teeth, read stories, and buckle them into the car? We often don't see all the teaching moments because they are kerneled into the everyday ones we walk so briskly past on our way out the door.

My oldest was born neurotypical, and while I spent many years doing things for him and then giving him bits and pieces to do on his own, it still took me by surprise when he stopped needing my help to get dressed, brush his teeth, get himself a snack, and buckle himself into the car. The day he came home from second grade, gobbling up a chapter book like a bag of Doritos, he left me speechless. How did we get here? I wondered.

Bit by bit and day by day is how.

Parenting a neurodiverse child is no different in that we play the long game, but it is different in every other way. We don't always get to take the same approach, and it often is a much longer game than expected.

When we first received our child's diagnosis, I felt as though I was at the base of that steep and rocky mountain, begging for it to be moved. But instead of the path leveling out and the mountain shrinking back, it rigidly held its monumental form, a thorough response indeed. And those first steps up the mountain were the hardest. Feeling I was leaving the safety of the world I'd only ever known behind, it was easiest to look back at first and long to go back.

But here's the thing about climbing a mountain: As you climb, you eventually lose sight of what is behind you, and where you started begins to look very small. It's as if the world at the base disappears, while the world around you becomes the only reality you now know as you climb higher and higher. And it's stunning, really, the way a mountain climb shifts your heart. The perseverance of the climb itself and the strength and confidence accumulated along the way transforms the heart, creating an undeniable truth.

That you can do hard things, even this hard thing.

This hard thing that you balked at before, that made you crumple in weakness and defeat, that made you angry and devastated, filling your heart with grief, turns out to have your name written all over it.

God, who has gone before you, carved this unique path just for you, knowing that the steeper and more challenging parts would stretch but not break you, and that the breathtaking beauty would captivate you in a way that spoke entirely to your soul alone.

A mountain that you once feared and grieved can become the bedrock of your new dreams—filled with the foundational strength, confidence, courage, and faith it took to climb that mountain. The very thing that we thought might defeat us has the very real possibility of becoming the thing that reshapes us, perhaps even the thing that equips us.

Climbing in Faith

One day, I had a revelation. By climbing my own mountain, I was getting pretty good at climbing mountains. I'd learned how to navigate the more complicated parts of the mountain; to rest when necessary or just when I wanted to stop and enjoy the view; to ask for help when I needed some assistance with a particularly tricky part of the climb; and to look back at the milestones along the way, celebrating each victory—no matter how big or small.

In this realization, it occurred to me that it's in our faithfulness where God strengthens and equips us. If I had stood my ground, way back at the base of this mountain, unwilling to step out and climb up in faith, I would have never been able to build my strength or confidence, nor find peace and joy as I faithfully made my way up.

In the Scriptures, we see God calling and then equipping, not vice versa. We see God's provision for the task He has called us to only by faith. Without faith, we won't ever take that first step, and we can't submit to the Lord and simultaneously hold tight to our ways. It does not work that way.

Before Abram became Abraham, before Noah built the Ark, before Esther was a queen who could influence a king, before David threw a stone at a giant, before Daniel sat among the lions and was not harmed, before each of the twelve disciples followed Jesus, they each had to take a step of faith.

While that step may have looked different for each of them, as it is for each of us, that step of faith is crucial to fulfilling the role He has set before us as moms. And what He calls us to, He is faithful to equip us for. But first, we must look up at the mountain He has ordained before us and, with faithful and trusting hearts, pick up our feet and move, knowing that God meets us where we are. Even if where we are is still at the mountain's base—the very one we've asked Him to move. Even when His answer is no, He's not moving it, He is still there to help.

But it's our step in faith, toward a mountain that won't be moved, that we must take, trusting that He is waiting for that step, eager to equip and fill us with everything we will need to make the climb. Trusting that His strength is there, waiting to fill us as we take that first breath of mountain air; that His peace will sustain us around every bend and switchback; that His joy will overcome us, with every breathtaking view and ray of sun that shines upon us; and that He is gracious, loving, and good, and has already mapped out the path, wanting us to trust Him with every direction and gain in altitude we are going to take.

Mountains don't always move; thank you, Lord, for that. I am forever reshaped and refined by them, and I now know that I'd never want to experience this life without this particular set of unmovable mountains He's called me to climb.

Grab Your Hiking Boots

Before my husband and I got engaged, he took me on a backpacking trip in the mountains. And for a girl who had rarely seen the inside of a tent before meeting him, this was a monumental step for me. And for us.

I was excited for the trip but entirely naive as to the level of physical exertion I was en route for. In the early miles of our hike on the first day, I held my head high as I gained confidence with my pack on. I enjoyed the scenery and took lots of photos, mostly of Craig's back as he hiked in front of me.

But as the day wore on and the miles added up, the pep in my step faded, and I grew weary and frustrated with how long the hike was taking. Each time I thought we were near our destination, I was met with an apologetic tinge to my husband's blue eyes as he encouraged me along, promising we were getting closer.

Ultimately, the hike took longer than I ever could have imagined and pushed me physically and mentally—more than I was prepared for. As our trek continued on, I asked for more stops, ate more of my snacks, shed unexpected tears, and even let my future husband carry my pack across a steep ridge of boulders, my exhaustion and fear of heights at an all-time high.

But along the way, something incredible happened. Just as we were cresting a hill, he stopped suddenly and swiftly put his arm out to stop me. No more than fifty yards away stood a stunning and massive bull elk. As he stood and stared back at us, I was in complete awe of his beauty. I had never been this close to such a large animal in its natural habitat. He eventually ran away, and I watched with amazement at such a powerful creature who could move with such grace.

Once at our campsite and fishing in a high mountain lake that likely had very few visitors of the humankind, we caught our fill of fish for dinner, witnessed an incredible mountain-top sunset, and then sat under the stars, feeling like the only two people in the world.

The next day, I proudly hiked back out and toward the truck. Smiling again, too. As I meandered my way through meadows and hopped over fallen logs, trailing behind Craig, I felt so grateful for what this mountain climb had held in store for me. Sure, it was hard, but it was incredibly worth it.

However, then we ran into wolves and after that, I pretty much ran the seven miles back to our truck and kissed the passenger door once we arrived safely to it. But that's a story for another time.

Sometimes we find ourselves on a climb we didn't expect—while other times we willingly take the climb, but then realize it's going to be much harder than we anticipated. Recognizing our weaknesses doesn't mean we've failed at the task. We're all going to get weary, fall short of expectations, take extra breaks, or trip and fall a time or two.

But keep going because there is beauty, majesty, and such memorable, life-changing views the further up we climb. In this journey, we can have both failure and success, hardship and joy, unexpected breaks and confidence in our steps. It isn't one or the other on the mountain; it's both. As it is on this rare and special journey we are on with our special needs children.

In God's creation, there are mountains, carved with unexpected obstacles and beauty. And they are always worth the climb.

Reflect and Pray

Queen Esther found herself in quite a predicament. A situation she likely never dreamed she would encounter was now staring her in the face. With her life and the lives of her people on the line, she faced a crucial decision.

I imagine it felt like standing at the base of a mountain that she felt ill-equipped to climb.

As a newly appointed queen, who was once a Jewish orphan, she would need to approach the king, be honest about who she really was, and ask for him to save her people from a decree that had been written to destroy the Jews.

Wise counsel came from her cousin, Mordecai, who said, "Who knows whether you have come to the kingdom for such a time as this?" (Esther 4:14).

Equipped with God-given courage, Esther took decisive action in order to save her people (Esther 7:3-4).

Be encouraged, knowing that God equips us for the steps He calls us to take. His sovereignty encompasses all things: every mountain you climb, every valley you traverse, and every breathtaking view you encounter are ordained for you. You are walking this journey, with its hills and valleys, for *such a time as this.*

1. What mountains have you asked God to move in your life?

2. Why might He move or not move them?

A Prayer for the Mom Standing Before the Mountain

Heavenly Father, I often grow weary as the path I climb feels steep and rocky. But I know that You go before me and have made a way for me.

Lord, I sometimes feel that I am standing before a mountain that I don't know how to climb, but I know that You will guide me in the ascent. I ask for You to guide me now as I navigate this unexpected but necessary climb.

Grant me the strength to endure and the courage to keep moving forward, even when the path is difficult. Fill me with Your peace that surpasses all understanding, and remind me that You are with me every step of the way.

When I feel overwhelmed and discouraged, surround me with Your love and comfort, and that Your power is made perfect in my weakness.

Help me to trust in Your timing and Your plan, even when it doesn't align with my own.

I thank you for choosing me to experience this life with my child and for all the joy that they bring. I ask for discernment on when to press on and when to stop and enjoy the view.

In the precious and holy name of Jesus, Amen.

CHAPTER NINE

Limitless Love & Unlimited Joy

I watched my one-year-old Jack struggle to take his own steps, regardless of how day after day we tried. For weeks, I continued to prop up my phone and tap the red circle to start the video, hoping to catch him taking his first steps as I gently held his fingers and prompted him along. But my fingers he grasped tightly, refusing to let go, and his wobbly legs gave out every time he tried to walk.

It wasn't how I remembered my oldest learning to walk. While we had yet to learn of Jack's diagnosis, something inside me scratched a mental mark, as if I was unknowingly keeping an internal tally of all the milestones he had missed and all the little things that might just add up to something more.

When we finally learned of his diagnosis, it all made sense, of course. Before his diagnosis, it felt as if I was trying to put the pieces of a puzzle together without seeing the finished picture on the box to guide me.

As I understood more of Jack's diagnosis, and the past became clearer to me, so did the future. Like a snake, the word "limited" slithered into my thoughts, whispering fear into them, preying upon my newly broken heart and crushed spirit. Despite my love for him, I saw the limitations my son would face, and it broke my heart even more.

Adding up all that I was reading, learning, and observing, it assured me of an unsettling conclusion: Those mental tally marks had already confirmed for me that my child had limitations.

Not the kind of limitations we all have, like my ability to run but never be a world-record marathoner or my love of singing in the car but my lack of actual vocal talent for achieving any fame or fortune. But the type of limitations that stop a person from doing many expected, typical child- and adult-type things.

My child might never play a sport like his peers, might never beam with pride while showing off his new driver's license, might never go to college, might never be in love and have the ability to get married and have children, and so on. I then had a bunch of "might-nevers" bouncing around in my head to prevent me from seeing anything but the potential limitations of my child's future.

While all those thoughts feel a bit archaic to me now, they felt so vividly tangible that I could almost taste the tears I would someday cry, weeping over all the milestones we always seemed to miss.

You might be there now, in the headspace of mentally batting away "might-nevers" like a pinball machine and wondering how my thinking changed. Well, as they say, time is a great healer of wounded hearts, and I'll add that it's also a great way to prove yourself wrong—at least in my case.

One day, Jack walked on his own. I don't think I have it on video, as I gave up trying to catch it on my phone sometime along the way. Then, one day, Jack learned to communicate in a way that better equipped him to ask for his own wants and needs instead of relying on us to guess all the time. The weight on my shoulders seemed to get a bit lighter after that.

One day, Jack learned some letters and numbers, and then could count to twenty and beyond. Another day, he was able to recite the entire alphabet. One triumphant day, he learned to ride a bike with training wheels. I proudly store that lengthy video in the archives of my phone.

One day, he potty-trained himself; another day, he dropped his echolalic communication and began having more organic conversations instead. Another day, he drew stick figures for the first time, and I snapped a photo of him smiling up at me from his little stick figure family while I let proud mama tears slip down my cheeks.

One day, he came home from school with a paper with his name scribbled in his handwriting. Another day, he came home from kindergarten excited to show me he had learned to skip. Not long after, he proudly pumped his legs and was swinging all on his own. And then, another day, he ran down our quarter-mile-long driveway.

I had placed limits on him, and then he blew those limits out of the water, showing me that he was not at all limited. Spending time with him, watching him grow, and seeing his limitless abilities have shown me I was wrong. But I am happy to have been mistaken.

Jack accomplished so many things in his own time and in his own way, on a path unmistakably marked for him that I was joyful to be a part of. As the days turned to months and months grew into years, I began to see a new future taking shape, and I could not wait to see what it held and all that he would accomplish. Instead of future, unshed tears of grief for the pieces of life we might miss, I felt the unmistakable swell of my heart for all the ways Jack would make me proud.

In my fears of what he might never achieve, I failed to see that I was the one limiting Jack by placing unsuitable ideals and expectations upon him. But along the way, in my journey's submissive faithfulness and mountainous climb, I realized that we were on an entirely new playing field, and he was boundless in his abilities here.

Finding Freedom and Redemption

Removing the "normal" expectations for our kids can be freeing. While we might operate by standards accustomed to the reality we know and understand, we must recognize that they do not. And it is a junction we all must arrive at—a crossroads where our original expectations meet the reality of what lies before us.

Perhaps, like me, you've sat and idled at this junction before, unsure if you could leave behind those original expectations or what awaited you if you did. My friend, I encourage you to breeze through that intersection, journeying to a place of peace and acceptance of your child's abilities. It's often tempting to look in another direction, wondering what it would be like, where so many others go. However torn we might feel as we motor toward something new and different, there is freedom in embracing it, too.

Since man was created, God has always given us a choice. And while we haven't always made the right choice—starting with Adam and Eve and that fateful day in the garden—God has always offered us redemption.

Our sins have never surprised God, and in His unrelenting love for us, He paid the ultimate price for our sins through Jesus (John 3:16). Through the cross, we are offered ultimate redemption, with the ability to live a kingdom life here on earth and an eternity with God. It changes everything, as we are no longer chained to death but instead set free.

The hope of Jesus—and His limitless love for me—changes me in every possible way.

When I think of the way I have perceived my son's abilities, or rather his inabilities, I am struck by how fearful and uncertain I felt, much like I might be without the hope of Jesus. However, in recognizing the unlimited potential for Jack's life and all that he will do, accomplish, and experience, regardless of how different it will be from what I once expected for him, I am filled with hope and a powerful purpose. A purpose that propels me forward with excitement for the journey ahead and all that awaits us.

As believers, we are never without the Holy Spirit—from the moment we accept Christ into our hearts, He dwells within us. As scripture says, "Now He who establishes us with you in Christ and has anointed us is God who also has sealed us and given us the Spirit in our hearts as a guarantee" (2 Corinthians 1:21-22).

Through the blood of Jesus, we are rescued and set free, unbound from the chains of this world. In giving our hearts and souls over to Him, we are also free from a way of life that limits our joy. Through Jesus, we can live a life full of joy, regardless of our outward circumstances.

In the years following Jack's diagnosis, we experienced several challenging seasons with him. I often felt like a hamster on a wheel, running the same track but never moving an inch. It always seemed that one challenge would be nearing its completion when the dawn of another one was just peeking over the horizon.

A Change of Heart

During one tough season, while we dealt with behavioral struggles with Jack, I often cried out to God in agony, feeling emotionally exhausted and overwhelmed, mentally at my breaking point and constantly begging for things to change. My prayers often sounded like this: "Please make Jack mature beyond this hard stage."; "Please make this easier for us."; and "Why is this always so hard?"

I remember shedding tears of frustration while begging and pleading with God to move the mountain for me. Of course, I knew I would be on a steep and rocky trek in my journey raising Jack, but this mountain suddenly felt too steep, too rocky, and too much for me to continue.

I wanted God to change my circumstances and work a miracle within Jack to make life easier. I hoped to see Jack grow beyond the deliriously hard behavioral challenges that made daily life with him such a relentless struggle. And while I waited God out, I grew angry, resentful, irritable, and bitter toward Him.

Hadn't I been here before? I had experienced such anger and frustration early on in Jack's life. What went wrong to bring me circling back to something I had once overcome?

My deceitful heart, of course. God never wavered in His promise to be with me, encourage me, and strengthen me. But I had wavered. Things got hard—again—and I again found myself shackled to my emotions, with anger and disappointment weighing me down.

Until one day, it all changed.

That day, I cried out to God, seeking His wisdom, not mine. My prayers were a cry for help, a desire for His guidance, a call to the strength that only He could provide, and a surrender to all of my ways.

His response was to move the mountain for me, but not at all in the way I had once begged Him to. Nothing about Jack's challenging behavior changed. Nothing about my situation was different, at least not from the outside.

Instead, the mountain that God moved, the miracle that He worked, was in me.

My heart was incredibly changed through everyday events orchestrated by the loving care of my heavenly Father. As if a veil had lifted from my eyes, and every wall of resistance surrounding my heart crumbled to nothing, I saw everything around me, including Jack and his unique struggles, through a new lens. What once irritated me was now giving me joy, and what I once fought against, I now embraced. If my heart and soul were a garden, God is the gardener set on extracting the weeds, granting space for joy and peace to bloom again.

What we often see as limitations, God sees as limitless possibilities to draw us closer to Him, changing our hearts through miraculous acts of love and mercy. In His infinite love for us, we are made new. We are new creations in Him, and our old selves are gone (2 Corinthians 5:17).

Philippians 4:13, which says, "I can do all things in Christ who strengthens me," often comes to mind when I think about what all my children might accomplish for themselves in the coming years. And while I may have once been guilty of sadness over what Jack might not or could not achieve due to his disability, it's through the changes God has worked in my heart and His healing over me that I can see the truly wondrous ways God will equip Jack for His purposes set before him.

His limitless love unshackles me from a life of frustration and fear, freeing me to enjoy a life of unlimited joy.

There is Joy in this Journey

At the beginning of walking this path, when we might be reeling from a fresh diagnosis, it might be hard to imagine a life free from frustration and fear and filled with joy instead. It might also be a monumental task to see beyond the limitations quickly tossed our way, along with a diagnosis. Like I once did, you might spend your first hours upon learning of your child's disability reading about all the things your child won't accomplish or be capable of in their life.

There will undoubtedly be things our kids won't do; however, there will also be plenty they are capable of, from the expected to the unexpected. Our children will surprise us in many ways, fill our hearts with pride and joy, and be the everyday miracles they are—the person who paves their own way in a world designed primarily for those different from them.

Walking this journey with our disabled kids is a unique kind of heartbreak, one that cracks it wide open for some of the most profound agony as well as the purest joy. It's breathtaking in both its hardship and in its beauty.

When I begin to fear for Jack's future, I am reminded of Psalm 139, a favorite scripture of mine.

O Lord, You have searched me and known me.

You know my sitting down and my rising up;

You understand my thought afar off.

You comprehend my path and my lying down,

And are acquainted with all my ways.

For there is not a word on my tongue,

But behold, O Lord, You know it altogether.

You have hedged me behind and before,

And laid Your hand upon me.

Such knowledge is too wonderful for me;

It is high, I cannot attain it.

Where can I go from Your Spirit?

Or where can I flee from Your presence?

If I ascend into heaven, You are there;

If I make my bed in hell, behold, You are there.

If I take the wings of the morning,

And dwell in the uttermost parts of the sea,

Even there Your hand shall lead me,

And Your right hand shall hold me.

If I say, "Surely the darkness shall fall on me,"

Even the night shall be light about me;

Indeed, the darkness shall not hide from You,

But the night shines as the day;

The darkness and the light are both alike to You.

For You formed my inward parts;

You covered me in my mother's womb.

I will praise You, for I am fearfully

and wonderfully made;

Marvelous are Your works,

And that my soul knows very well.

My frame was not hidden from You,

When I was made in secret,

And skillfully wrought in the

lowest parts of the earth.

Your eyes saw my substance,

being yet unformed.

And in Your book they all were written,

The days fashioned for me,

When as yet there were none of them.

How precious also are Your

thoughts to me, O God!

How great is the sum of them!

If I should count them, they would be

more in number than the sand;

When I awake, I am still with You.

(Psalm 139:1-18)

This is a favorite scripture of mine for multiple reasons, primarily because it calms any anxiety or doubts growing within me. How wonderful it is to know that God loves me like this, to know me better than anyone else.

Also, it is incredibly wonderful knowing that God loves my kids this way! What a comfort it is to know that God knows everything about my son, Jack, even the things that I do not. I may not know all of Jack's capabilities, but God does. I may not know Jack's future, but God does.

There are no limits to what God can do, and no one person is without value to Him or His kingdom. As any proud mama would be, I imagine God's incredible plans for Jack, a future full of hope and plans beyond the limits of my imagination.

We must cling to God's promises, trusting that all things are made new in Him, from our very own hearts to the paths set before us and our kids.

Through God's infinite love and our hope in Jesus, our limitations do not define us, and joy is truly within reach.

Reflect and Pray

David came prepared to fight Goliath with just a handful of stones. It seemed an unlikely weapon of choice and yet, Goliath was defeated. David's faith in God, greater than any weapon, was all he needed to overcome the giant who towered over him, even though he was only a shepherd boy at the time.

King David, as he would later become, was courageous, a good leader of the people, wrote many of the psalms we know and love, and is a part of the lineage of Jesus. He also made mistakes that are recorded in the Scriptures, ones that caused heartache and loss. Regardless of his sin and flaws, he had a beautifully intimate relationship with God.

God doesn't need our perfection; He just wants us to love and trust Him. He wants us to show up with what we have and allow Him to do the rest.

King David wrote, "Commit your way to the Lord, trust also in Him, and He shall bring it to pass" (Psalm 37:5). Wise words coming from someone who knew God so well and Scripture has referred to as a "man after God's own heart" (1 Samuel 13:14, Acts 13:22).

When we impose limits on ourselves and our children, it's like we are placing limits on God, the Creator of the Universe, who once spoke to Job, saying, "Have you commanded the morning since your days began, and caused the dawn to know its place?" (Job 38:12).

Let us trust in He who commands the morning that He can work through any obstacle we or our children face.

1.   What limits that your child may face are you worried about?

2.   How might God work through your child's limitations to fulfill the beautiful and unique purpose He has called them to? With this new perspective, how do you now feel regarding the limitations your child will face in this life?

A Prayer for the Mom Who Desires Love and Life Without Limits

Heavenly Father, I come before You today with a heart full of love and a spirit yearning for Your boundless grace.

Lord, grant me strength when I feel weary and peace when I am overwhelmed. I know that the value and worth of my child are not measured by worldly standards, but by Your infinite love and grace. Help me to keep this truth tucked boldly into my heart, no matter what challenges my child may face.

Lord, I ask You to break down any barriers of doubt, fear, and limitations that might hold my child back from fulfilling the purpose You have called them to. And fill our hearts with unwavering faith, knowing that with You, all things are possible.

I ask that You surround my child and I with a supportive community that understands, uplifts, and encourages us.

I ask for guidance in finding joy in the small victories and in embracing the unique journey we are on.

In the precious and holy name of Jesus, Amen.

CHAPTER TEN

Faithfully Resilient

Arms and back aching, I gently lowered Jack into his crib. He was finally asleep. And as I let him go and watched his little body relax onto his mattress, I felt the heaviness and the hardship of the day drain away. Silent tears, heavy with grief, slid down my cheeks; it had been a tough day of his relentless crying.

Before this moment, with evening upon me, the familiar dread mixed with relief crept through my veins, spurring adrenaline borne of nerves for what lay ahead. I was about to embark on the task of putting Jack to sleep, something that would take all my strength when my strength was nearly gone, as he entered his fussiest time of the day, after already crying for most of the day. When he was finally asleep a few hours later, I felt like I had run a marathon of the heart and soul. Feeling crushed by the task itself, I wearily bounced and swayed, rocked, and shushed until he was asleep in my tired arms.

As I stood there, towering over his crib, I felt as though my worn-out feet had grown roots into the carpet, and I was unable to move, regardless of how I had longed for this moment in the hours before. It was a hard day on the tail of weeks of hard days, and I was beyond exhausted in ways I had never experienced before. And yet, I stood, rooted to the spot, adoring my baby boy as he slept soundly.

While I let those tears slip, they seemed to water something within my worn-out soul. Looking down at my sweet baby boy, my heart and thoughts echoed in unison with an undeniable truth that swelled like the climb of a song toward its chorus—an anthem my heart beat vigorously to, no matter how wearisome the day had been.

I would do this for you over and over. Again and again. I will always do this for you.

With those words still thrumming through my soul, I felt God's presence wash over me, and on the next beat of my heart, His words replaced my own.

As I would retake the cross for you.

It was a mere moment, but it cracked open the darkness surrounding me, shining light into what felt hidden and isolated. Jesus was meeting me there, in my darkness, as I wrestled with the conflicting emotions that fought to rise within me. And just like a sea He had quieted before, the storm within me ceased. And in the quiet, there was peace.

Unbeknownst to me, the resilient love I felt for my son that evening as I stood over his crib, shedding tears, would only be the beginning of what I would endure and how resilient I would learn to be.

From those early days with my fussy baby to feeling shattered by grief in the months post-diagnosis to the challenges I face now, there is a foundation on which I've built my resilience. Bricks of faith lay at my feet, supporting me from the ground up.

If we imagine our faith like a house protecting us from the elements, then we can easily see how important it is to have one with a solid foundation, sturdy walls, sealed windows, and an impenetrable roof. Would an unfailing love for my child be enough to keep us safe from the trials and tribulations this world would blow our way and rain down upon us? And was my love enough to shelter us from the storms of life? Or was my faith what kept us secure and safe, regardless of the hardship pelted at us?

While my unconditional love for my child kept me marching forward along my journey, regardless of the terrain or the ominous storms that lay in my path, I was still rocked by grief, tossed in its waves without rescue. The daily challenges often tripped me up along my trek, sending me stumbling backward, retracing steps I'd already taken. And sometimes, when the path was incredibly steep and the storms substantially intense, I found myself hanging on for dear life, making no forward movement.

My faith in the Lord is what tethers me to true strength and safety. He is the house that shelters and never fails to provide for me.

Growing in Faith

One evening in late spring, after tucking my three children into their beds, I escaped outside for a moment to myself. My husband was still in the house for anyone needing "one more glass of water."

It was the kind of spring evening that blurs the line between spring and summer, and longer hours of daylight were on the horizon. As I strolled through the yard, leaving behind the toys strewn about from the day, I wandered into the fields surrounding the house, my sandals catching grass with every other step. And with the rhythmic slap of my sandals against the soles of my feet, I was reminded of an evening like this but entirely different.

I've shared this evening with you, the one when I practically fled from the prison-like walls of my house after several days of an unrelenting sickness reigned within. Exhausted and burnt out, I was ready to yield to my emotions but instead was met with God's grace and perfect peace—recharging my weary soul in a way only He could.

I recalled that evening as I took the same path I did then—this time with an entirely new perspective. It had been a year since I had stood in that field and felt exhaustion radiate from hair tips to fingertips. It had been a year of growth—for me, my family, and my faith.

As I strode further out, chasing the last rays of sunlight, desiring that heavenly, golden glow to wash over me, I realized I was more faithful and resilient than ever. What God brought into my life, He had seen me through it as well. Considering who I was early on in this journey until now, God's faithfulness in equipping, strengthening, and drawing near to me is most evident in my life.

As someone who grew up in the Christian faith, I hadn't always known the Lord this deeply. While I'd always known Jesus as my Savior, now I knew Him as my friend. Along the path of this journey that He set my feet upon, I had begun to take His hand more and more, not just in a way someone might do for survival but out of a desire to be near Him and know Him more. I had long wondered how others had developed such a deep, friendship-like relationship with Jesus, and now I knew. By reaching for Him daily, I then never wanted to let go.

As I stood in the green, grassy field, bronze sunlight danced through the towering pine trees behind me, I thought more about what had changed, or rather, how I had changed. As my mind traced its way back through the years, I could recall many things I did right and wrong as I journeyed along this path and grew my faith in Jesus.

How could I—myself—have brought about such a radical change at a heart level, especially as I battled the daily struggles of raising very young children and the unexpected challenges of raising a child with a disability? It was out of my sphere of abilities to conduct such a miraculous shift at such a deep level within me. So, if not for my own doing, where did such a monumental alteration originate?

Jesus.

He is my Savior, my friend, my Redeemer, and my miracle worker. He has been working in me since the beginning, playing the long game as He planted seeds that would take years to bloom, not at all surprised by my wrong turns, pitfalls, or blunders.

When we spend time with Jesus, we want more of Him because He first wanted us (1 John 4: 19-21). Our hearts long for Him in the way a child longs for their parent or a flower reaches and opens toward the sun—He is our Creator and home. And He is the reason our hearts change.

It's why some people can go to church but still not have faith—because it's not about us. It's about Him. If He is in our hearts, then things like church, Bible study, Christian music, books, devotionals, and fellowship will impact us and help us grow in our faith. But if He isn't in our hearts in the first place, then those things are like bad soil and will not yield a crop. No amount of Christian-like works, or actions, can change a heart quite the way Jesus can.

Before I returned to the house, I took one last look around, delighting in the peaceful quiet of a late spring evening. And the beauty of it all struck me—both the view spread before me and the entirety of my story—how God had orchestrated all of it for my good and His glory. Even the hardships, challenges, and grief had another side to them. Through God, none of it was wasted.

My mistakes weren't the end of the road as it had sometimes seemed. Redemption was always around the corner.

The hard seasons gave way to better and easier ones, and bursts of joy colored my days, as if wildflowers bordered the path on each side.

The grief will always ebb and flow, but instead of being tossed and tumbled along its waves, I am anchored to an immovable peace that will forever hold steady in a storm.

God's immeasurable faithfulness took my broken heart and healed it better than I could have myself. I am more faithful than before and more resilient for the path ahead—a life transformed with a new heart—that started with brokenness.

This reminds me of the apostle Paul, who was a devoted persecutor of Christians before he began his ministry. But all of that changed one day when he was on the road to Damascus and was stopped by the appearance of Jesus, who had already been crucified. You can imagine the terror Paul (who went by Saul then) must have felt! The book of Acts covers this incredible conversion and how Paul—a sinful and broken man—was entirely transformed by Jesus.

While we may not all have as radical a conversion as Paul's, we can appreciate the picture it paints of how Jesus changes hearts and lives.

And because I love a full-circle moment, let's jump back to the Old Testament when the prophet Ezekiel mediates between God and the Israelites.

"I will give you a new heart and put a new spirit within you; I will take the heart of stone out of your flesh and give you a heart of flesh" (Ezekiel 36:26).

What God promises, He fulfills. And this promise of a new heart has been changing hearts for a very long time. From the Israelites to Paul to me and, I hope, to you.

From one once-broken heart to another, trust God to work a miracle within you and then be prepared to be led on a path of redemption and transformation that equips you with the faithfulness and resilience your brand-new heart desires.

A Faithful and Resilient Mama

As a person who loves to plan ahead and rarely waits to start a new project, I'm never at ease in a situation that requires me to wait. I'm always thinking ten steps ahead and chomping to get going. In a waiting season, I quickly become impatient and am eager to find a new route to reach my desired destination. If a roadblock were to turn up in my path, I would not be the type to sit down and enjoy the wait. Instead, I'm like the Google Maps navigator who quickly says, "recalculating," and I'm scrambling to find a new way.

As many of us are acutely aware, our special needs kiddos take us on unexpected journeys with custom timelines, and we don't always have an estimated arrival time to our next destination. Also, I don't do well with waiting.

So when life pitches me a detour, and it's the long route of which no amount of recalculating can speed up, I might spend most of my time looking for ways to knock the roadblock over, get around it, climb over it, or dig underneath it. I never considered just sitting and leaning against the detour, resting along my journey, or enjoying the scenery where it has stopped me. And pretty soon, as I've pounded the pavement enough to drive myself crazy, looking for an alternate route that is nowhere to be found, I'm exhausted, frustrated, doubtful, and mad, feeling like a hostage in my current situation.

My inability to control my circumstances steers me off course. It always happens when life's storms blow me over, and I am not in my safe place, with a roof over my head and walls to protect me. We might often say, "Jesus, take the wheel," but at some point, we all tend to say, "I'll take it from here." And when that happens, we all realize what terrible drivers we are.

As I've grown in my faith and walk with Jesus, I've learned repeatedly that He knows what I do not. Whether I'm waiting out another challenging season or awaiting test results that have my anxiety in overdrive, leaning deeper into my faith and trusting in Jesus brings me peace, especially with my son's diagnosis.

Trusting in His timing is hardly ever easy, but between the Bible's first and last pages, there is an abundance of reasons why I can trust Him. Reading scripture reminds me of God's faithfulness, grace, mercy, and love. And as a child of God, there is no better place for me to be other than right in the middle of His plans, regardless of how well they fit into my schemes or schedule.

This is why I often tell myself the same thing over and over.

He knows what I do not.

Maybe He's rerouting me to keep me safe, or instead, it's to teach me something.

Regardless, I trust that He is building me to be more faithful, more resilient, and exactly who I'm meant to be.

My friend, as you sit amid a challenging season, feeling defeated by the weight of your circumstances, lean into Jesus and know that what God has called you to, He will see you through.

"And we know that all things work together for good to those who love God, to those who are the called according to His purpose" (Romans 8:28).

He's called us to be faithful and resilient mamas for our little ones and the road we walk for them. So trust that He will equip us to be exactly that.

A faithful and resilient mama.

Reflect and Pray

"Therefore we also, since we are surrounded by so great a cloud of witnesses, let us lay aside every weight, and the sin which so easily ensnares us, and let us run with endurance the race that is set before us, looking unto Jesus, the author and finisher of our faith, who for the joy that was set before Him endured the cross, despising the shame, and has sat down at the right hand of the throne of God" (Hebrews 12:1-2).

Jesus endured the cross, with joy.

And it's hard for me to even find joy in washing dishes some days. But that sure does put it into perspective, doesn't it?

He endured the cross with joy because it was His purpose here on earth and the will of the Father.

From this very scripture passage, we are called to "look unto Jesus" as we run our race. Meaning, we are to live like Christ as best we can.

What does God have in mind for you as you run your race? If you aren't sure, pray for wisdom and clarity as He reveals it to you.

1. **What does it mean to you to be a faithful and resilient mama?**

2. **What do you think God's purpose is for you, and how can you fulfill it with joy?**

A Prayer for the Mom who Desires to be Faithful and Resilient

Heavenly Father, I pray for a heart full of faith and resilience as I step out boldly in this role that You have called me for.

I pray that You will continue to transform my heart in a way that more and more aligns with where You need me to be to fulfill the purpose You have called me to. I ask for the presence of Your joy and peace to be a foundational part of who I am in You, so that I may do all things with the joy and peace of Christ.

Grant me an unwavering faith, Lord, to trust in Your plans, even when the path is unclear. Fill me with Your strength and resilience, enabling me to face each day with courage and grace.

Help me to find joy in the midst of trials and peace in the midst of chaos, and to remember that even the small, everyday moments are seen and valued by You.

*I thank You for the gift that is my child and all that they bring
to my life. I thank You for choosing me to be their mom, and I
am so grateful for the incredible blessing that they are to me.*

In the precious and holy name of Jesus, Amen.

CHAPTER ELEVEN

Hope in Eternity

The gravel crunched beneath my feet as I pushed the stroller, while a blue sky radiated above us as my daughter and I slowly made our way down the driveway, where the bus would soon meet us. At eighteen months old, she was entering an era of independence and often preferred to walk on her own during our afternoon treks to pick up her two older brothers from school at the bus stop.

It was early fall, and the necessity of the light jacket I wore seemed to come and go in rhythm with the sun as clouds chased away its warmth now and again. We wandered up and down, stopping to look for rocks or sit down and play in the dirt. As she played, my mind drifted. My Sunday school class had begun a study on heaven, and it had tugged free an idea buried in the fibers of my thoughts. What would Jack be like in heaven?

From what the Bible teaches us about heaven, we know that every tear will be wiped away. No longer will we experience death, mourning, pain, or sadness. All of these things will have passed away (Revelation 21:4).

Scripture regards the kingdom of heaven as a place of incredible joy and peace, free from the burdens of sin, death, decay, and suffering. Therefore, I can only imagine how joyous it will be to meet my son when he is free from his mental and physical disabilities.

That day, I walked the driveway, waiting on the afternoon bus, and imagined what that heavenly greeting might be like. I was not able to write it down at the time; I wrote it a few months later. I was shocked at how much I had retained, and I wholeheartedly believe that God preserved it for me so that I could one day share it with more than just the open blue sky, the whispering breeze, and the clouds above. He wanted me to share it with you.

The following is fictional, of course, but I hope it fills you with hope—for what incredible joys await us in eternity.

Meeting Jack in Heaven

My time on earth is done, and I'm walking through a heavenly meadow, arm in arm with Jesus.

The view is breathtaking in its beauty and familiarity. In all my years on earth, I'd never walked through anything like it, yet it has a strong sense of home as if I'd always longed for it.

Up ahead, someone awaits us, and as we draw nearer, this person takes a somewhat familiar shape.

I know exactly who he is, but he is not as I knew him. The marked differences between who he was then and what I see now bring a rush of goosebumps to my skin. I'd always wondered what he would have been like if he had been born with all his chromosomes. It seems as if I'm about to find out, and I am shaking in anticipation of this long-awaited greeting. My heart leaps with the realization that I am about to meet my son, in some ways for the first time.

Jesus grips my hand in understanding and then lets me go so I may walk toward him myself.

He is tall and in the prime of adulthood, like we all are here. I can see his shoulders—straight and strong—their droop, specific to his earthly condition, is gone.

As I get near him, I am overjoyed to see that his eyes are the same blue and his hair has a slight curl. So, he did inherit his blue eyes from his dad and the wavy hair from my mom, a heavenly revelation that lights up my heart.

The nose is different, but I recognize it to be more like mine than we ever saw in our earthly days.

His face resembles what I remember but has a restoration that overcomes my soul. This is what he would have looked like, bringing me to the fullness of joy.

In his eyes, nose, chin, cheeks, and smile, I can see myself and my husband, a blend of us and bits of others, but wholly himself, a face we saw but in shadows, never fully glimpsed in our earthly days.

In how he holds himself before me, I see a handsome, strong, confident, capable, loving young man. I see a quick wit, boundless energy, and unparalleled love for others—all things we witnessed on earth—now set free to fulfill exactly what he was meant for.

I glimpse a complete understanding in his eyes, and it speaks to my heart, as if to thank me for all I did for him when he could not.

I cannot wait to talk with him now that all delays and disabilities are no longer a barrier, and I am filled with the joy of what I once knew as a child on Christmas morning, but this is so much better.

Words hang between us as I am now within arm's reach of my son. I am smiling, and the most indescribable joy blooms in my heart. I have never felt like this before. There is no room for sadness, fear, doubt, anxiety, or grief.

The fullness of joy has wiped them from thought, feeling, and existence.

"Jack."

His name is barely a whisper as I grapple to find words amid my awe. His smile broadens at the sound of my voice, and I hear one of my favorite words again, now for the first time in heaven.

"Mom."

And we embrace, pulled together like two magnets bound together by an earthly, and now heavenly, lifetime of love and devotion. And then, like a drive-in movie, all the good and precious that was ever between us plays before us.

I was holding him on my chest minutes after he was born, and we locked eyes for the first time.

It's the night after he had screamed all day, and I've finally gotten him to sleep for bedtime. I'm bone-tired, and my soul is weary, but as soon as I put him in his crib, an incredible love fills my soul. I look at my precious baby boy and know in my heart I'll do this again and again for him. I saw something I had never seen but somewhat felt at that moment: Jesus was standing there with me and looking at me in the same way, with unconditional love and compassion for my heavy heart and struggles. He had drawn near to me when I needed Him most.

Jack is now trying to walk, and it's taking him longer than I remember it taking with his older brother, but we keep at it. We practice and practice, and I continue to praise him for each wobbly step. Before we know it, he astonishes us all by running through the house and playing "ready, set, go" with his older brother. A famous game they would play just before bedtime where they would line up at the door and then race through the house, around a chair in the living room, and then back to the same door to do it all over again. The images that dance before us bring big smiles to our heavenly faces now as we watch Everett race ahead and then see Jack as a toddler, curls bouncing on his little head, proudly running after his big brother.

We receive his diagnosis of William's Syndrome, and while it is soul-crushing, it is equally relieving. I wonder how I will handle it all. The grief, the unknown future. But ultimately, an unearthly peace fills me, and I march on into this new role. Determined to do all that I can for him.

He is four, and we dance in the kitchen. His arms are wrapped around me, and he has the biggest smile on his face. Little did I know then, but now I am fully aware that the simpleness of my embrace alighted his soul.

It's the middle of the night, and he is awake from a bad dream. I am there to soothe him. I can feel the peace and comfort from my touch and my presence. He drifts back to sleep.

We are driving home from another medical specialist appointment, just he and I, and I am worried. Thinking of all that might happen, I turned the radio to K-Love, our favorite Christian radio station, and as I sing along with the familiar songs, my heart is softened with peace, and I lift a hand in praise. I soon catch a glimpse from the rearview mirror of Jack's hand lifted in the air as well, as he sits strapped into his booster seat. We share this moment in silence. I wonder if he could ever comprehend, and I think about a day when he will. A day when we are both in the meadows of heaven.

One scene after another, from some of the biggest moments of our lives to all the simple, seemingly mundane moments, plays before us in the air. Each one is good, special, and precious to us both.

From toddlerhood to high school graduation and beyond, I am reliving the joy of the journey with Jack as his mom, and it feels like a celebration. There was so much hardship, grief, and fear, but none of that remains. Here, on the other side of heaven, it has all been redeemed. It was all worth the effort, even on the hardest of days or the longest of nights. It was all for so much more than IEP meetings and EKGs; it was bringing the joy of God to the world through us both. Through all the fears, the grief, and the lifetime of joy, it was always about bringing glory to God.

We stand proudly together, arms wrapped around each other as the final scenes of our earthly life play before us. And for the first time ever, the full glory of God around us, the full knowledge of why we were given those earthly roles (like a gift before us now), all the questions such as the "why me" or "why him" are answered, and we are wrapped in the love of Jesus with His words echoing in our ears, "Well done, my good and faithful servants."

And as I lay my head on Jack's shoulder, the fullness of joy and contentment overwhelming my soul, he whispers gently into my ear,

"Well done, my faithful and resilient mama."

My Hope for You

"For our light affliction, which is but for a moment, is working for us a far more exceeding and eternal weight of glory, while we do not look at the things which are seen, but at the things which are not seen. For the things which are seen are temporary, but the things which are not seen are eternal" (2 Corinthians 4:17).

A moment.

Temporary.

As I read this scripture passage, my eyes could not help but snag on those words. In truth, it's hard to imagine this life being anything but a mere moment, but then again, I can't quite wrap my mind around eternity either. I am used to beginnings and endings, life and death, health and decay. Yet, the Scriptures' promises highlight eternal glory for us—one without the trials, tribulations, adversities, sickness, death, and sins of this world. Can you imagine a life without illness, without pain, without death, without ... disabilities?

"And God will wipe away every tear from their eyes; there shall be no more death, nor sorrow, nor crying. There shall be no more pain, for the former things are passed away" (Revelation 21:4).

The Bible clearly states that there will be no pain, sorrow, or sin in eternity. The most beautiful visions fill my mind as I sit with that knowledge. All that seems lost will be gained: all health, all knowledge, all abilities, all joy. And on a day much like any other day, I was given a the vision of meeting my son in heaven, the beginning of our eternal lives in the kingdom of God, surrounded by His glory. This vision gave me incredible hope, not of this world or my limited days on this earth but of what is beyond it.

Back on earth, as I walked my driveway, tears wetting my cheeks, waiting on the school bus that day, I felt God whisper to my heart, like the wind blowing softly against my cheek.

Yes, you will see him like this one day, too.

As the scenes of what I imagined played in my mind, I felt God's voice breathe through the winds again.

Share this with others. They need to know.

He's right. We need to know that this world is not the whole of our story. There is an eternity for us, and if we place our hope in and submit our hearts to Jesus, the most beautiful parts of our stories are yet to come.

While I tread along this journey, with its unyielding climbs, harsh climates, and breathtakingly beautiful views, I am hopeful about what lies ahead for me. The trek strengthens me, and I look back to recognize how God equipped me for each step. I am purposeful in my journey, gratitude filling my heart as I steward the task set before me, renewed in each moment by God's presence and my unconditional love for my child.

Now that you are on this journey with me, too, I hope you've found a friend and noticed the multitude of those who walk beside you.

As we journey, I hope you find strength in each new step.

Peace along your path.

Joy as you climb.

Hope for what is up ahead.

And most of all, my friend, I hope you see Jesus here with you, too, matching your steps, forging ahead for you, lighting your path, sheltering you from storms, giving you rest, and offering His hand when it is too much to bear.

I hope that in Him, you find an indestructible faith.

I hope that with Him, you find the strength for all this journey brings.

And I hope that through Him, you discover this solid, unshakeable truth:

You are not alone.

Reflect and Pray

For the followers of Jesus, immediately following His death on the cross, hope felt lost. With their Messiah buried in a tomb, feelings of grief, confusion, and anger must have consumed them.

And yet, we joyfully shout, "He is Risen!" every Easter Sunday.

Hope was never lost—God had a plan for redemption and restoration all along. Three days after the darkest day they could have ever imagined, the disciples stood face to face with a resurrected Jesus and finally began to understand.

Like the disciples, we are going to struggle with understanding the plans of God, especially when we live in a world that plagues us with sin, pain, loss, death, disease, and disabilities. But God is bigger than the brokenness of this world; in fact, He has overcome it.

We may not understand why His plans are the way they are or why He allows what He does here on earth, but we can be certain of His infinite love for us. We can secure our hope in Him because He planned to rescue us all along. And through the cross and the sacrifice Jesus poured out for us there, there is bountiful hope for us now and in eternity.

There is hope—endless, beautiful, radiant hope for each one of us.

"For God so loved the world that He gave His only begotten Son, that whoever believes in Him should not perish but have everlasting life" (John 3:16).

1. In scripture we read that heaven is a place without sin, death, sickness, or sadness. In light of the struggles we face in this life, how do you feel about experiencing the freedom of heaven one day?

2. Imagine meeting your special needs child in heaven, and they are free of their disabilities. What might that look and feel like?

A Prayer for the Mom with a New Heart Full of Hope

Heavenly Father, I come before You with a heart overflowing with gratitude and hope. Thank you for the newness of life You bring, for the hope that springs eternal in Your promises.

Thank you for breathing fresh life into my spirit and for filling me with Your joy and peace. May this newfound hope be a beacon of light in my life, guiding my steps and filling me with courage.

Father, as I embrace this season of hope, I pray that You will continue to help me to see Your hand at work in my life, orchestrating every detail for my good and Your glory.

Grant me wisdom and discernment as I navigate the challenges and joys of motherhood.

Surround me with a supportive community that celebrates with me in times of victory and lifts me up in times of need. Lord, may my hope in You be unwavering, rooted deeply in Your unfailing love and faithfulness. Strengthen my faith and help me trust in Your perfect timing and plans for my life and family.

Thank you, Lord, for the gift of hope that You have poured into my heart. May it overflow into every aspect of my life, bringing transformation, healing, and joy.

Thank you for planting an eternal perspective within me and for reminding me that raising my children and nurturing my family has eternal significance.

In the precious and holy name of Jesus, Amen.

Afterword

"To everything there is a season, a time for every purpose under heaven" (Ecclesiastes 3:1).

As moms, we often refer to different times in our motherhood journey as seasons. There is the newborn season where sleepless nights, exhaustion, baby snuggles, and milk-stained shirts reign. There is the toddler season, the school-age season, and the teenager season, and tucked into each of those are seasons within seasons. Like the season of sleep regressions, potty training, play dates, after-school sports, etc. All with their own unique ups and downs. And while all that makes up a particular season doesn't last forever, when we are in one, especially a challenging one, we are often tempted to believe otherwise.

As I wrote this book and reflected on the early days of my post-diagnosis season, I was reminded of what has changed and stayed the same and, most of all, how grateful I am for seasons. Grateful for what they have brought, taught, and, often, that they don't last forever.

The season I am in now is certainly different from the one I reflected on while writing this book. Since receiving Jack's diagnosis, Jack attended two years of a developmental preschool that did wonders for him; we welcomed a daughter we named Claire; we've moved once and have another move on the horizon; I got serious about writing my first book; my husband had two career changes; I now have two out of my three kids in school; we added chickens and, much to the disdain of our cat, a dog to our lives. and even a goat, although Curly the goat wasn't with us for that long.

All of that to say, *life* moved on. Where I once felt stuck on the hamster wheel of hardship when I was caring for a colicky baby and busy toddler, wondering when life would feel normal again, I eventually realized that all of those long days and sleepless nights piled up and, day by day, we left one season for another.

I once felt stalled by grief, stuck in the heaviness of it, my life seemingly halted by what I had least expected. I never imagined I could move forward again and greet all of what lay in wait for me. When I felt weak under the weight of grief and the impact of this diagnosis on our lives, I couldn't yet see that this season of sorrow, sadness, and perceived weakness was actually preparing the way for growth, joy, and strength.

Not because of any miracle of my own doing but with Christ in me. *He is the miracle worker.* Scripture teaches us that God's strength is made perfect in our weakness (2 Corinthians 12:9). It's God who transforms us and His strength that equips us for the hard seasons yet to come. Where we are weak, He is strong; therefore, *with Him*, we have everything we need to handle all that comes (Philippians 4:13).

This season I am in now is not easy, and while we still navigate the challenges of Jack's diagnosis, I feel a distance between where we started and where we are now. When I first learned of William's Syndrome, I grieved the loss of what I had always hoped we'd experience with Jack—all those future hopes and dreams I had for him. But through processing my grief and getting to know the hope of a new future, I stumbled along something else unexpected.

Acceptance.

I have come to accept Jack's differences, even the ones I've yet to know. His ways are uniquely his own. What once triggered the sting of grief no longer has such a vicious hold on me.

Since Jack's diagnosis, he has seen many specialists, including neurologists, nephrologists, endocrinologists, cardiologists, ophthalmologists, audiologists, speech therapists, occupational therapists, and physical therapists.

And while his initial round of specialist appointments was a lot to bear, we now see fewer specialists each year. And even though I've found peace when it comes to many of these appointments, there are still some that trigger anxiety when I see them ahead on the calendar.

A month after we received Jack's official William's Syndrome diagnosis, he was also diagnosed with Supra Valvular Aortic Stenosis (SVAS), which is what many in our William's Syndrome community also face. His diagnosis with SVAS has been moderate, and he meets with his cardiologist every 3-6 months to keep an eye on it. If his condition worsens, he will likely need heart surgery.

Heart surgery feels like a black cloud that I often see in the sky, off in the distance, and I wonder if it's a storm I will one day have to weather with him. My fears grip me even harder as I brace for what might come because, for Jack, surgery is a risky, complicated matter. Anesthesia, necessary for surgery, can be life-threatening for those with William's Syndrome, and we don't know why. My mama's heart pounds a little louder every time I wait for the cardiologist to come into the room after each echocardiogram, trying to read his eyes with any sign of bad news he might be carrying with him that day.

Jack was also diagnosed with ADHD just before he started kindergarten, at no surprise to any of us. This was one diagnosis I was anticipating, for once, and instead of being shocked and dismantled, I felt prepared and expectant, ready to add it to the list and use it as a tool to understand my son better.

I've discovered something else since those early days as well. The more I know about my son, the better prepared I am to help him thrive. It's like packing for a vacation. If you check the weather beforehand, you can bring the appropriate clothing and plan relevant activities. But if you plan for sunny beach days and only bring swimsuits and flip-flops for your beach getaway, but it rains the entire time, you'll be sorely disappointed.

I've had plenty of days when I didn't know what to do for my son, and we felt stuck in survival mode, not at all enjoying it either. But the more I have leaned into *who* Jack is and *what* he needs and doesn't need, what works or doesn't work, the better prepared I am for each day.

When the hard days pile up, I am mindful that it's just a season—one that God has been preparing me for, step by step, long before I ever stepped onto this special and unique path.

In fact, God's fingerprints have been all over it even when I was completely unaware.

I find immense comfort in knowing that God is with me and has been with me throughout the difficult days and challenging seasons. And what a comfort to know that He will walk me through every valley, every storm, and every difficult climb that this path holds for me.

What began as "the end of the world as I knew it" has since been lovingly and skillfully transformed, and God has knit together a beautiful story that I'm grateful to be a part of.

As my Good Shepherd, He has comforted me, led me to peace, given me rest, and restored my soul just as the Scriptures say He will (Psalm 23:1-3).

I'll be honest: The sting of the reality of raising a child with a disability and encountering twists and turns in a way I never imagined does still rock my boat and likely always will. Grief will come and go; new fears will threaten my peace; the anxiety of his future will be a constant shadow in my mind; the potential for risky but necessary surgeries will continue to loom overhead; and the lack of true independence, for either of us, as he will likely live with us as an adult will always be a part of my story.

If you're reading this with a fresh diagnosis and you're heavy-hearted, wondering when it gets easier, I can't give you an exact timeline, as all of our disabled children are different from one another. But I will say this: With time and their own growth, the picture gets clearer, and we can better understand them, which does help immensely. Their disabilities might become more distinct, and so may their abilities. And watching them participate in something they love or practice a skill they have mastered is another level of joy you didn't know existed.

I hope that my personal stories, reflections, and what I've shared from scripture have given you a newfound or reconfirmed understanding that your heart *will* heal. The heavy weight of grief does recede, but it's important to grieve and allow yourself the time and grace to do so.

Being a mom is the most rewarding and challenging thing ever. Being a mom to a child with a disability is a different level of challenge, and while it certainly has its own incredible rewards, it's something I often grow weary of experiencing. Long after the pain and shock of the initial diagnosis has subsided and everyday life feels like a marathon of parenting battles, it is so easy to feel defeated.

I am certainly in that season now, and it is hard. But I am not alone. I do not go unseen, unknown, or unloved as I climb my way through this particularly steep leg of my journey.

God is with me for every step I take. So, I will keep clinging to Him, finding peace and strength in His presence and His word. And I hope you do, too.

Whatever season you are in as a special needs parent, know that you are doing something that few do or understand, but God does. He's given you this role for a reason, and as you care for your child and steward the task set before you, He is glorified and honored.

And in each step you take along this journey, He is with you.

With love,
Erica

Acknowledgments

To my husband, Craig, who told me years ago that I would write a book. Those words have echoed in my ears ever since, and I knew, without a doubt, that you would fully support me when the time came. It turns out you were right, and so was I. I wrote the book, and you wholeheartedly supported me. Thank you for believing in my abilities and encouraging me along the way. Thank you for being an incredible husband, best friend, and partner in this life. You've taken on the role of "special-needs dad" in ways that inspire me, and I am so grateful to have you by my side as we navigate a path we never imagined we would take. In hindsight, God was preparing me for the road less traveled since the day I met you when you swept me off my feet after a hike along the Grand Ronde River. Thank you for taking me on outdoor adventures and backpacking into the mountains. God knew I needed those experiences and, most of all, that I needed you. I love you.

To my mom and dad, who have always been my biggest cheerleaders. Your support, encouragement, prayers, phone calls, and long talks have always been a pillar of love and support in my life. Thank you for creating a home and life built upon faith in Jesus Christ. Thank you for diving into the special needs world alongside me and being such incredible grandparents to my kids. You've always made me feel seen and loved, and the comfort of your presence is always near whenever I feel alone. I love you both so much. Thank you to my church, Sunday school class, and Bible study group for your prayers and encouragement for this project. I am so grateful for the love and support you have all shown me.

To Ben and Havilah Cunnington and Havilah's Author School writing coaches and staff. Your author school was exactly what I needed even though I wasn't looking for it. It undoubtedly helped me level up as a writer and cross the finish line. Those four months changed my life, and I'm eternally grateful for your wisdom, love, prayers, and encouragement. Thank you.

To Heather, Louise, and Veronica, the "Waterproof Mascara" mastermind group. I'm grateful to have walked through the process of writing our books together. Your honesty, feedback, and vulnerability gave me the courage to keep going, week after week, chapter after chapter. I love you all!

To my editor, Blair Parke, thank you for taking on this project and guiding me through the editing process, making it fun, and being an incredible resource. I'm so grateful for your essential part in this project, thank you!

Thank you to the Havilah's Author School Publish Like A Pro team for taking my words and creating something beautiful to hold in my hands and share withthe world.

To all of my dear friends, close family, and prayer warriors who have prayed over me and this project, I'm grateful for your love and support.

A special thank you to Clare, who delivered the toughest news I've ever received in the most caring of ways. I'll always be grateful for you.

To all the special needs moms that have gone before me and now walk beside me. You all inspire and encourage me. Thank you for boldly and bravely sharing your stories, reminding us all that we are never alone.

And to my children, Everett, Jack, and Claire, you are my greatest treasures and more precious than anything I could ever do or have. Thank you for the gift that each of you brings to my life. I love you in the morning and in the afternoon. I love you in the evening and underneath the moon.

Reference Page

Cooke, George W., "I've Got the Joy," hymnary.org, originally written in 1925; accessed on August 8, 2024, https://hymnary.org/text/i_have_the_joy_joy_joy_joy_down_in_my_h

Kingsley, Emily Perl, "Welcome to Holland," emilyperlkingsley.org, 1987, https://www.emilyperlkingsley.com/welcome-to-holland

William's Syndrome Association, "What is William's Syndrome?" williams-syndrome.org, accessed on August 8, 2024, (https://www.williams-syndrome.org/what-is-ws.org)

.

www.ingramcontent.com/pod-product-compliance
Lightning Source LLC
Chambersburg PA
CBHW061743120626
46550CB00005B/1877